"Jennene's personal story in *Overthrow* is a living testimony of God's grace and redemption, rescue and restoration. She gives light to those living in the shadows of death feeling deep shame wondering if there is hope for them."

— MAC AND MARY OWEN,
Celebrate Recovery National Directors

JENNENE EKLUND

Foreword by Cheryl Baker

Over throw

LUCAS LANE

Published by Lucas Lane Publishers
Designed by Nicole Grimes
Edited by Meredith Hinds

Printed in the United States of America

First Edition 2017

10 9 8 7 6 5 4 3 2 1

Library of Congress Cataloging-in-Publication Data
Eklund, Jennene, 1976–
    Overthrow: How to unseat the false king and live in victory/
    Jennene Eklund.
        p. cm.
    ISBN 978-0-9964747-3-3

Dedication

To my husband, who turned on a light in a dark room.

Contents

Foreword ix

Preface xiii

Chapter 1 **TREATMENT** 17

Chapter 2 **SHAME** 27

Chapter 3 **DO YOU WANT TO GET WELL?** 37

Chapter 4 **A DIFFERENT PERSPECTIVE** 47

Chapter 5 **THE ROOT OF THE PROBLEM** 59

Chapter 6 **THE USURPER** 73

Chapter 7 **HAVE YOU EVER FELT THE EARTH BREATHE?** 89

Chapter 8 **SPIRITUAL WARFARE** 101

Chapter 9 **PREPARING TO FIGHT** 107

Chapter 10 **WAR** 125
Have I Identified and Declared War Against the Enemy?

Chapter 11 **THE DEFINITION OF HAPPINESS** 133
Could I Be Happy If I Never Lost Another Pound or
Could Never Alter My Physical Appearance In Any Way?

Chapter 12 **MIRROR, MIRROR** 145
Am I Looking at the Mirror Inside as Much as the
Mirror Outside?

Chapter 13 **UNSPEAKABLE** 161
What Am I Doing With Feelings That Are Too Much
to Bear?

Chapter 14 **TWINKLING OF AN EYE** 179
            Am I Pursuing a Perfect Body or a Perfected Body?

Chapter 15 **REFORMATION** 197
            Am I Using Food the Way God Intended?

Chapter 16 **THE LATE USURPER** 215

Chapter 17 **THE BEGINNING** 229

Epilogue 243
Postscript: Through My Husband's Eyes 247
About the Author 259

Foreword

Ten years ago, I met Jennene and her husband, John, at a Celebrate Recovery Conference in Ohio. Over dinner that evening, Jennene seemed shy and insecure, often letting her husband do the talking. I found myself wondering about what could have caused this beautiful, young woman to be so quiet and serious? What hurts from her past made someone, who seemed to have it all, become so withdrawn and anxious?

Over the years, I have had the privilege of seeing, up close and personal, the transformation that has occurred in Jennene's life. She is now a courageous, confident woman who loves to laugh. The changes she has made in her life have strengthened her bonds with her four daughters. One of her goals has been to break the cycle of dysfunction in her family and her success is evident in her strong, talented and creative children.

She is now a pastor's wife serving in North Carolina. She loves sharing her testimony and mentoring women. Most importantly, she wants to share the hope that she has found through her Savior, Jesus Christ.

I am very proud of the work that Jennene has done to find victory over her hurts, hang-ups and habits. In this book, she shares the troubles of her past and her journey to healing. Her life story, illustrations, scriptures, and path to a new, joy-filled life will be inspirational.

— CHERYL BAKER,
Co-Founder of Celebrate Recovery

For I consider that the sufferings of this present time are not worth comparing with the glory that is going to be revealed to us. For the creation eagerly waits with anticipation for God's sons to be revealed. For the creation was subjected to futility—not willingly, but because of Him who subjected it—in the hope that the creation itself will also be set free from the bondage of corruption into the glorious freedom of God's children. For we know that the whole creation has been groaning together with labor pains until now. And not only that, but we ourselves who have the Spirit as the firstfruits—we also groan within ourselves, eagerly waiting for adoption, the redemption of our bodies...

ROMANS 8:18-23

Preface

Christmas was coming soon.

Preparing for the holiday's festivities meant gift buying and giving, baking and decorating, being inspired by projects seen on Pinterest, and subsequently being embarrassed by the outcome of attempted projects discovered on Pinterest. My mind was filled with little girls wearing velvet dresses adorned with plaid taffeta and satin bows, handcrafting ornaments, and singing songs with child-like wonder about the sweet baby Jesus, lying in a manger.

In the midst of such merry happenings, I found myself, the mother of four young daughters, performing daring feats of hair-styling acrobatics wedged in our undersized upstairs bathroom, surrounded by beadboard and peeling paint. It was the night of the annual Christmas play. As most parents can testify, conversations in such situations can be amusing, they can be informative, they can be entertaining, and if extended long enough, they can lead to episodes of pent-up sibling violence.

"Mommy, I love you more than the sunset and the sunrise," said my youngest daughter, Rose, as she attempted to hold my hand, which at that particular moment, brandished a blazing hot curling iron. "I love you more than a big heart in the sky. A big heart that is sparkling." She paused for dramatic effect. "I love you more than all the penguins in the world."

Her three older sisters burst out in peals of laughter. Rose's brown eyes narrowed in moral outrage, the tender sentiment expressed not two minutes before instantly forgotten. The barrette she was clutching was about to become weaponized.

I quickly tried to steer the conversation in a different direction. "So, what part are you playing this year?"

"I'm an angel," Rose said angelically.

"Weren't you an angel last year, too?" Violet inquired with the air of one in a parliamentary debate.

"No," Rose replied.

"Well, I'm sure you were an angel last year."

"No—I was a shepherd last year!"

The oldest, Daisy, a ten-year-old fountain of factual knowledge, rebuffed. "Girls aren't shepherds. Besides, I remember you wore the white angel costume last year because we could see your underwear through it. They were pink with white hearts."

The tension mounted yet again, and Lily, the second oldest, intervened. She excelled in the art of distraction through changing the subject. "Well, I remember that I was Holly in the play last year. But I really wanted to be Noelle, the street-smart orphan with a talent for rapping," she said.

"Excuse me," Daisy quipped, "did you really just say 'with a talent for wrapping'? As in wrapping presents?"

"No. Rapping. Like this."

She proceeded to perform "Here We Come A-Rapping among the Leaves So Green," and I began to panic. I was sinking into the realization I had absolutely no memory of that play. My brain was frantically reenacting the events of the past year—I should remember such a thing! I was their mother, after all. I organized and cataloged every moment of their sweet little lives. It was my job, my joy, my greatest pleasure to remember momentous occasions. I searched my memory over and over again, fruitlessly.

What could be the cause of such a glaring short-term memory loss? Had I been in a coma? Had I undergone a lobotomy?

My fingers stopped moving as I searched for these memories.

What were they wearing? What did they sing? Who played the lead? Who was awarded the solos . . . ?

A wave of dawning comprehension hit: I didn't remember it because I wasn't there.

CHAPTER 1

Treatment

Jesus wept.
JOHN 11:35

In November of 2009, I entered an inpatient treatment facility for women with eating disorders. I would love to be able to say that I went nobly and willingly for the good of my family, but that was not the way it went down. My husband gave me an ultimatum: Either I had to enter treatment, or things were going to be very different. I would no longer be able to live at home and subject my children and family to the tyrannical dysfunction that was my existence with an eating disorder.

I certainly didn't want to go. I was ashamed that I had let my life come to this. Shame was as natural as breathing. Guilt had ravaged promise, leaving the person I dreamed of being buried under the ash heap of despair. I had been struggling with an eating disorder in one form or another for decades. At that point, it was all I knew. I knew it as assuredly as the sun moves in an unrelenting arc across the sky from east to west. And I was desperately scared of what my life would look like without it.

Yet, deep inside me, there was a longing—a longing deeper than the ache of excruciating hunger—for a life without the constant fear of food. If treatment worked, maybe, just maybe, I could really be free. I wouldn't have to mark occasions in my life by how much I weighed on that particular day, or if I had been able to make it through the day without eating. I wouldn't have to retreat to my bed to deal with the physical aftermath of bingeing and purging.

I wouldn't have to keep telling my beautiful little girls excuses for why I wasn't eating: that I was just really tired, really sick, really full, really busy. I wouldn't have to see the disappointment in their eyes when I said I couldn't attend one of their games or concerts or dance classes because I didn't feel well. I could be liberated of my reluctance to take them on a picnic at the park because I couldn't handle being around food. We could go on long walks, bike rides, dance in the rain, play badminton in the backyard, explore unknown paths together, without me feeling like I was going to black out.

The decision to enter inpatient treatment, which would entail me packing up and flying across the country, was truly a last-ditch effort. I had managed to evade the ignominy of "going away" for almost twenty years. But at that point in time, there was truly no other recourse. I could either go through with it, or I would surely lose everything; my children, my family, and I would all become just another sad statistic.

I hung all my hope of recovery and a "normal" life on what I would learn while I was in treatment. Far away, out of sight and out of mind, they could fix me once and for all. After all, places like that existed to fix the unfixable, to warehouse all the dysfunction and human wreckage that assaulted the average person's way of life. At least, this was how I felt. And sadly, that was where the avalanche of my poor decisions and devastating pain had carried me. There was no plan B. I had tried it all. I decided to go, morbidly consoling myself that if this didn't work, nothing ever would.

I gathered every ounce of resolve I possessed and kissed my sweet girls good-bye while they slept. The house was deadly quiet, my telltale heart the only sound I could perceive. I felt that if I even whispered, the pounding of my heart would overcome me, and I would not have to strength to do what I was required to do. And so, not daring to breathe, I watched my daughters sleep.

A remarkable and magical transformation occurs in the eyes of a parent when their children fall asleep. As their faces relax and their breathing settles into the familiar rhythm of slumber, it is then a spell is cast. They appear once again as they did when they were very, very small, when their every breath was a wonder to behold, when the miracle of life was plain, etched in the features of a tiny babe asleep in sheltering arms. On the night of my leaving, the softness of their long-ago faces appeared as I watched them sleep .

I kissed them again in the darkness of the early morning, the sky so black it seemed that the stars were hiding their faces. I boarded a plane as the sun rose over a motherless world for my children. As the plane gathered altitude, my determination began to crumble. I felt loneliness and resentment spread through my soul like a disease. I was alone and cast aside. Didn't everyone realize that I had really been trying to get better? Why couldn't they see and appreciate all my efforts?

I had tried and tried and tried. And failed and failed and failed. Yes, I was keenly aware of the trying and failing. It was so incredibly hard—food was All-Pervasive . It was everywhere. The inundation of food in our culture is truly unimaginable. How could I ever escape its omnipresent reach? Every moment of our lives is marked by food; we feast our lives away, moment by moment, and food is everything.

Why couldn't anyone see *that?*

What they saw instead was an abomination. Some struggles you can wear on the inside and shadows keep them hidden. But to struggle with food? How many times did I hear . . . how many times did I tell myself, "Don't you know that your body is a temple of the Holy Spirit?" Didn't I know that the way I treated my body was displeasing to the Lord? Didn't I know that I was squandering a life of God-given health? The obvious answer was yes . . . I knew it better than anyone.

However, nothing could compete, nothing could even come close to convincing me that those things were more important than being thin. Thin was all I ever knew. I was thin and thin was me. I couldn't give up my identity. Didn't everyone know that if I weren't remarkably thin, then there was nothing remarkable about me?

I wrestled with those agonizing thoughts while squeezed into the middle seat on the airplane, desperately trying to avoid contact with the passengers on my right and my left. They were immersed in their own doings: watching the movie, reading a book. They were passing time in their own normal lives. How could anyone do anything normal while I was sitting there, my world falling apart? No, I don't want anything to drink. Please, move your knee; don't touch me. Don't look at anyone; don't make eye contact or your heart might break.

Finally, the moment arrived to disembark the plane. I had previously been informed that someone from the treatment facility would be waiting for me at baggage claim to give me a ride. As I filed off the plane, I comforted myself with the thought that I would at least have a moment to gather my composure between exiting the plane and being picked up by the treatment worker in baggage claim. I *needed* that moment to come to terms with what was about to happen to me.

I stepped from the gate and entered the terminal, steeling myself to begin the death march from freedom to imprisonment. To my horror, I was face-to-face with a woman holding a sign with my name on it in big, black letters. I felt utterly betrayed. This wasn't supposed to be happening! Inside I was seething with anger, *How dare she stand there so insolently? Wasn't it a criminal offense for her to be here? Where was Homeland Security?*

She stood, not ten yards from me, holding my name in her hands, JENNENE EKLUND scrawled in black maker across a flimsy piece of paper.

A wave of shame engulfed me. Rage suddenly gave way to incomprehensible sorrow. I began to sob.

She might as well have been holding a sign that said "failure as a mother."

I was sure that at any moment they were going to attach a scarlet letter to my clothes. I clutched my jacket closer to me and followed her, crying uncontrollably, stricken with grief as we paraded through the terminal. We collected my suitcase and began the hour-long drive to the treatment center. Looking back, I am sure that she was very kind and professional. She attempted to engage me in conversation; but I could never remember what we talked about. I was consumed with sorrow, resentment, and militant fury. I was in deep mourning for all that I had been forced to give up: my children, my marriage, my home, my self-respect, and most importantly of all, my eating disorder. I knew that it was killing me, but I needed it to manage life.

I couldn't imagine life without the constant presence of hunger.

When I arrived, I realized there had been a monumental mistake. I did not belong in this place, filled with women and girls with feeding tubes. They were all around me, some standing, others sitting around a large round table with food in front of them. Treatment workers were stationed everywhere. The room was covered in dark wood paneling, and the fabric on the furniture was dark brown. Everything was brown. Colorless and oppressively brown. It was a bright sunny day, and I felt like I had just entered a tomb. My stomach revolted. I didn't want to touch anything.

A woman sitting at the table was struggling to open a package of M&M'S, her frail limbs shaking with the strain of the effort. She finally succeeded, and the colorful contents spilled out all over the table. Gathering them up, she methodically placed them in front of her on a napkin. Under the watchful eye of the treatment worker she began to eat them, one at a time, at the speed of a great land tortoise. The girls around her were encouraging her,

"Great job! Look at you go!"

I watched the scene, looking from one person to another, wondering sardonically if they realized they were treating her as if she were a sideshow at the circus. *Come one, come all, and behold the lady who eats a package of M&M'S. The plain ones, not the peanut kind!*

May God have mercy on anyone who tries to talk to me like that, my thoughts blistered. A treatment worker led from me that room to another small, clinical-looking one in the back. I was handed a hospital gown to put on. Gritting my teeth, I complied. The nurse performed a battery of tests, utilizing numerous medical devices, including multiple needles. But the most horrifying experience of all was being weighed. She did not allow me to see what the number was. I was convinced, in my much maligned delusion, that the nurse and the treatment workers took great delight in withholding that particular information. They watched me angrily putting my clothes on as though I were a caged animal, a spectacle at the zoo, existing for the delight of those who had the luxury of casually regarding me.

From that moment on, my feelings about being in treatment could be defined in one word: *rage*. I watched with hatred as a treatment worker searched my belongings, rifling through my suitcase and purse, piling what was unsuitable in the middle of a table on display for all to see. I felt my heart breaking as she unceremoniously deposited four little stuffed animals, tenderly chosen and sent along with me, in the "not allowed" heap.

"People do dangerous things with them. You can't even begin to imagine what people think to do," the worker said as I lunged for the only remaining link to my children's existence. From there, she led me to yet another small, clinical room to be "psychologically evaluated." Degradation, humiliation, and shame were filling every fiber óf my being. What in God's holy name was happening to me? I wrestled with deciding if I should tell them what they wanted to hear or what I was really thinking and feeling.

Reason convinced me that telling them what I thought they wanted to hear could potentially get me out of there sooner.

Throughout the course of my life with an eating disorder, I had certainly been to my share of counseling sessions. I knew that disturbing song and dance. I took great pride in the gift I believed I possessed to manipulate any situation. It was always the same: The therapist would sit across from me with a condescending look on her face, or from time to time, pity. She would force me to relive the past, searching for the deep-seated, dark secret, the reason I had so many unfortunate tendencies. It was always a pointless endeavor. I already knew what my problem was: I weighed too much. If she would just leave me alone, I could lose those five more nagging pounds that were the elusive key to my happiness.

When this evaluation was completed, the treatment worker released me back into the large, wood-paneled tomb. I surveyed the filthy couch, searching in vain for a blanket. But blankets, like stuffed animals, were too dangerous for us to be trusted with. Pillows, however, appeared to be innocuous objects and were plentiful. Piling pillows on top of myself like a funeral pyre, I curled up in a ball and sobbed.

I thought I had prepared myself for what it would feel like to be separated from my children. But nothing, *nothing*, could have prepared me for the violent, visceral reaction I experienced as the reality of the separation assaulted me. I felt as if I couldn't breathe. God had truly forsaken me. I had begged countless times for God to take this eating disorder away from me, even going so far as to

swallow my pride on one occasion and ask a group of church elders
to lay hands on me and pray.

God could remove it instantly; I knew He could. So why didn't
He reach down and rescue me? I had inflicted so much physical
damage on my body. Why did He not heal me? I had petitioned
and pleaded so many times before. As I lay on that couch wallow-
ing in my wretchedness, I cried out in desperation one last time.

God, have mercy on me! Help me!

I sat up, pillows tumbling. The heavens were silent. The room
around me buzzed like static on a radio, with the activity of all of
those sick women. And I was one of them. My heart hardened to
bitter steel, and defiance came over me such as I had never known
before. A battle cry stirred in my soul; there was no one, not even
God Himself, who could force me to do what I did not want to do.
With that attitude in my heart, I readied myself to face the treatment worker who was coming over to my couch to tell me it was
time for dinner. Dinner. A showdown, the first of many, was about
to start.

Since it was my first meal there, I was given the great privilege
of sitting at a table for two, a treatment worker and myself. In
retrospect, I can see it as a practice designed to ease the transition
of the incoming resident into a new behavioral pattern. A pattern
that involved eating. I looked across the table at the worker and our
eyes locked. I was on the warpath and she was in my way. I would
not let her tell me what to do. I would not let her turn me into an
object of pity.

Three other large round tables, filled with women, were within
arm's reach. Being separated yet still surrounded only further reinforced the feeling of being a spectacle on display. I could feel their
furtive glances as I sat staring resolutely ahead with the plate of
food in front of me—food I was going to have to eat. I couldn't talk
my way out of this one. In a businesslike tone, she told me to take

off my jacket because it had pockets in which I could potentially hide food. My hands were to be visible on the table at all times, so that she could make sure I was eating every morsel of food that was on the plate. There was half an hour to eat it all. Or else.

The clock started and the stares coming from the other tables intensified. I could practically hear their brains humming with thoughts. *Would she eat? Would she refuse? What will they do if she refuses?* That was the one question I needed answered. What would they do if I refused?

I picked up a fork. The fork had been specially engineered to be safe, with blunt tips and edges. I guess they figured I wouldn't be able to hurt myself with it. Didn't they know there were so many other ways in which I could hurt myself?

I put the fork in some Jell-O, which appeared to be the least calorie-laden food on the plate. Lifting it to my lips, I ate a tiny, mouse-size bite. It tasted so good. I didn't often allow myself the luxury of tasting food because hunger was my preferred state of existence. And while I liked being hungry, and was always in a state of hunger, going hungry was by no means an easy feat. That was why it was easier to not eat. Food tasted so intoxicatingly good, and once I started eating, it was agonizingly hard to stop.

I swallowed the Jell-O and put the fork down in a display that announced I was done eating. Through a dazzling display of self-control, I had proven that I had mastered myself, had shown them that I was in control. In defiant irreverence, I felt like I had just shouted my battle cry for all to hear. *"Look at me! No one can make me do what I don't want to do!"*

CHAPTER 2

Shame

The mass of men lead lives of quiet desperation.
HENRY DAVID THOREAU

Up until the point I entered treatment, the fact that I struggled with an eating disorder was a secret I was determined to take with me to the grave. The hard edge of the constant need for lying had worn down the softness of my conscience. Conscience was a fickle friend, anyway. I couldn't rely on it as much as I could rely on my eating disorder. Conscience had led me to trust that others could help me, and the repeated destruction of that delusion brought with it immense wreckage. And the cost of repairing all that damage was a price too high to keep paying.

Lying came very easily to me. I had a practiced answer to every pointed question. I was a pastor's wife, after all. I was not supposed to have problems. I dressed the part, worked in the nursery, taught Sunday school, did whatever was asked of me; for the love of God , I even knew how to play the piano, which was a virtual prerequisite of being the spouse of someone in ministry. If I was struggling, I needed to keep it quiet, keep it a secret.

My actions were measured against this standard: don't make a fool of yourself, your family, your church. The expression "living in a fishbowl" could be ascribed to my life as a pastor's wife at that time. People felt as if they knew me and my children because of my husband's role in the public eye. On the rare occasion I felt safe enough with a person to be able to start to disclose that I was dealing with an issue involving food, their immediate response was usually enough to stop me in my tracks. These encounters reinforced the belief I held that I would only be met with judgment if I revealed what was really going on.

Only once, at that time, can I remember someone actually attempting to identify with my struggle. I really admired this person. She always seemed to have compassion in her eyes; she was on the prayer team and was a doer of good deeds.

I don't know what I expected would come of sharing the fact that I had an eating disorder.

I began to confide to her, "I just can't make myself eat. I get so terrified and overcome with fear that I will become fat if I let myself eat." I quickly looked down. I didn't want her to see how much it had cost me to be that vulnerable. This beautiful woman looked at me with genuine love and concern.

"I know what you mean," she said. "There was one summer in 1987 when I was not able to keep anything down that I was eating. It was awful."

My heart fell into my stomach. I knew I should have kept it to myself. Her best, most empathy-filled effort to relate to me only served to redraw the boundaries of my isolation. Her response didn't cause me hurt, and I don't fault her one bit; she was truly trying to love me. But one thing became more and more clear to me with every passing encounter: my affliction was of a new breed. Drinking, using drugs, even sexual wanderings, were deemed very, very bad, on the list of very, very bad things, and were just cause to be unwelcomed from a church. But they were also known quantities. An eating disorder, however, would elicit a response like this: "What the hell is wrong with you? (Yes, a church person actually said this to me.) Just eat!" Or "Stop making yourself throw up!"

I was a pioneer in a brave, new, dysfunctional world; a world riven by shame and misunderstanding. People at church, even the most well-intentioned, were simply unequipped to deal with me.

THE NUMBERS TELL THE STORY

According to South Carolina Department of Mental Health, eight out of ten thirteen-year-old girls have reported dieting to control their weight. *Eight out the thirteen-year-old girls think they need to lose weight!* These are girls who want to be loved; who want to be seen as beautiful and special; who believe they are not good enough.

In the college age group, 91 percent said that they have already dieted. Over half of teenage girls have used unhealthy behaviors to control their weight. These behaviors include skipping meals, fasting, smoking, vomiting, and taking laxatives (Neumark-Sztainer, 2005). According to the *International Journal of Eating Disorders,* 13 percent of women over the age of fifty displayed eating disorder symptoms. These include fasting, skipping meals, excessive exercise, laxative abuse, binge eating, and self-induced vomiting. Seventy percent of this age group is actively trying to lose weight and 62 percent felt that their weight and body shape had a negative impact on their life.

These are the statistics. These are the facts. Percentages and numbers tend to reduce things to emotionless, scientific figures. But the truth is, they represent real people. People like your thirteen-year-old daughter who quietly goes to youth group every week.. People like your grandmother who sings in the choir. People like your sister who volunteers in the nursery. People like you. People like me.

And these statistics barely scratch the surface of what is going on in the hearts and minds of women and men who are likely to be sitting in the pew on Sunday morning. Many of whom have eating disorders. Or at least a very tortured relationship with food and how they feel about their bodies. Week after week, they sit, suffering in silence. They don't look the part of a person in pain. No one asks. They never tell.

The vast majority of those who struggle with food don't look emaciated. Personally, the times I was at a normal weight were the most hellish. I engaged in disordered behaviors, but I wasn't noticeably thin. I couldn't even manage looking like I had an eating disorder! If I had asked for help, who would believe me?

"You look fine to me," they'd say.

Inside I'd cry, *I'm not fine! Do you want me to spell it out? Do you require I give you every nauseating detail? Every flashback? Every crippling fear? Every insecurity? Do you want me to brand the word DAMAGED on my flesh so that I can be forever identified as the failure I am?*

But that was what people required, it seemed. And I did not want to give it to them. I would rather die than give that to them.

I was not alone. I've been in countless confidential support groups, and in my experience, these statistics are a small reflection of the real numbers. People feel that they would rather go to their graves than ever let another human know what they have done. And what has been done to them.

I remember the day a woman, who was closer to my mother's age than mine, approached me at church. She asked if she could share a secret with me. I prepared myself to hear a scandalous confession. Instead, she whispered, barely able to form coherent words, her voice strangled in shame.

"My son died in a freak accident. I can't get over it. And now I can't stop bingeing and purging. He'll never come back. Never. I hate myself for what I do." Her features twisted in anguish. "Promise me you will never tell. No one can ever know."

One of the bravest men I have ever known told me about the first time he worked up the courage to tell someone at his church that he was bulimic. They openly mocked him.

"Are you serious? Only young white girls have eating disorders! What kind of a freak are you?" News of his struggle spread like wildfire thanks to a prayer request chain. "Did you hear about Brian? He needs our *prayers*." The reaction he received convinced him that church was the last place on the face of the earth he would find compassion. Let alone help.

And so, the hurting trudge forward in silent pain. No one will ever know that Brian wants someone to reach through the blackness and help him, that Brian was molested when he was a kid, that Brian's father left, that Brian has hopes and dreams.

The nameless, faceless numbers of the unreported swell, rising in a shameful tide. Its unrelenting waters beat against the doors of the church.

I WANT TO REMEMBER

Perhaps some churches have someone on staff who is willing or qualified to do some counseling. I know there are many pastors who spend countless hours with hurting parishioners. I have seen the multitude of these people, filing into a pastor's office, hoping to not be seen by another congregant as they enter the room of unholy disclosure. But more likely than not, someone with a deep hurt is referred to an outside secular resource to get better there. And while motives vary widely, damaged people are sent out to be "fixed" so that they will then be capable of reintegration into the church. There is a disconnect between the church's professed desire to reach out and their willingness or ability to actually deal with people who need help.

It's admittedly messy business. And unfortunately we are inundated with a religious culture that has turned "Go , therefore, and make disciples of all nations" into "If we build it, they will come." Offering real help to someone else might mean they have to confront their own shame and shortcomings . . . and besides that, they just don't know *what* to do. The church as a whole is often at a loss to offer practical, "in the trenches" solutions and counsel to those with deep-rooted, significant issues and pain.

If someone is drowning, whether or not they wandered unnecessarily into dangerous waters, is the appropriate response to yell from the shore, "You should have known better!" or "Why don't you swim back to shore and then I can help you!"?

If one of my children carelessly fell into the water and was being swept away, you had better believe that I would jump headlong into the waters to rescue them at any cost. Jumping in to save someone who is drowning involves getting in over your head. It involves extreme risk. The decision to help, to rescue, to save a drowning life, means swimming out to meet them and by any and all means necessary returning them back to shore.

Many times, the church would rather toss out a life preserver in the general direction of the victim, leaving it up to the sinking soul to grab hold. I had a lot of Bible verses hurled at me in life preserver fashion as I gasped for air and flailed. As I was being pressed down under the overwhelming waters, they threw platitudes at me which usually contained the phrases "Reaping and sowing" and "O ye of little faith" and the previously mentioned "Do you not know your body is a temple?" They flung verses from the holy book of My Own Ridiculous Opinion: "God helps those who help themselves," "You've made your bed, now go lie in it," and my personal favorite, "Just get over yourself."

I have had many, many encounters with church people who thought it was their job to determine my fitness for the ministry based upon my weight and too-thin appearance. I have been taken to lunch for the express purpose of letting me know that the way I treated my body was not pleasing to God. My husband has been told, more than once, that he was a failure as a spouse because his wife was hurting so much. They quoted Christ's words to him,

"Physician, heal thyself" (kjv). Any advice that was offered amounted to this: Just believe what Christ had done is enough and *move on with your life.*

Honestly, I *did* believe that what Christ did was enough. That was exactly why I felt like such an unmitigated failure. I beat myself up with some of the same questions.

> "If I believed that Christ's death on the cross was my cure, why am I still sick?"
> "If by His stripes I am healed, why am I still hurting?"
> "If Jesus paid it all, why do I feel so spiritually bankrupt?"
> "If Christ came to set the captives free, why am I still living as in bondage?"
> "If Jesus rose from the dead in triumphant victory, why am I living in defeat?"

Was the issue with me? Had I gone too far? Had I done too many bad things that I was now beyond the reach of the Cross? Had I so abused the grace of Jesus Christ that I had used up all of my chances? Had God finally had it with me?

For as long as I could remember, shame was a force greater than and as irreversible as gravity. It kept me trapped under the weight of condemnation. It kept me viewing the beautiful, sacred truths of Christ's love and forgiveness as nothing more than the mile markers of failure on my long, pitiful, scandalous road to death.

Shame is a parasite. It will attach itself to anything if it is given the opportunity. It sucks the life out of grace and twists it into guilt. It preys on things that are wholesome and pure. Anne Rice wrote, "Why does shame and self-loathing become cruelty to the innocent?" It does not matter where the shame and loathing came from or for what reason they developed. They overtake the innocent without mercy and with supreme malice.

In this way, shame overwhelms the little one who thinks she is insufficient because of some careless thing a bully has said. It overwhelms the middle-aged woman who looks in the mirror and convinces herself that because she let herself go, her husband walked out. It overwhelms the young man who feels defeated because a faceless religious person posted something on social media that mocks his struggle. It overwhelms the mother who can't stop bingeing and purging while her children play in the next room. It overwhelms the young woman who gives herself to men who don't love her, convinced she is not worthy of love because of how she looks. It overwhelms the grandmother who sings in the church choir, standing at the edge of the group, hoping no one will notice how grotesque she has let herself become. It overwhelms the teenage girl as she tries to starve the life out of the pain of the memory of being abused.

Shame is suffocating. How can one possibly begin to contemplate living a life of purpose and happiness when every breath is a struggle to survive?

There are some moments when I myself am sick and tired of thinking about and telling my own weary, old story of shame. It is not who I am anymore. But then God reminds me that it is not my story anyway; it is His story, and He has entrusted me with it. Corrie ten Boom said , "Every experience God gives us, every person He puts into our lives, is the perfect preparation for a future that only He can see." And shame was a masterful, brutal preparation for me. Living a life of shame was, to me, a fate worse than death. It was a dementia of the soul that imprisoned me in a perverted truth of what my reality was. I knew that distorted condition well. I pray I never forget it, either.

I need to remember it. When I remember Christ's bitter suffering, I don't remember for the sake of the sorrow, but for the sake of what that suffering accomplished: redemption and eternal life. In the same way, I will keep on remembering and sharing my own story of shame because right now someone is lost in the shadow of dark disgrace, and it is a dark shadow, indeed. But shadows can only exist where there is light. This means that while we may feel lost in the shadow of death, light is ever present.

So hold on. The light is fast approaching, and when it finally breaks within your soul, you will be filled with hope and with life made all the more brilliant because you have walked through the dark shadows of shame.

CHAPTER 3

Do You Want to Get Well?

From the beginning, men and women have sought to
free themselves from this crushing human predicament.

RICHARD FOSTER

I recently listened to a podcast about a man named BJ Miller, formerly the executive director at the Zen Hospice Project in San Francisco. He suffered a terrible accident at age nineteen when he was electrocuted. The trauma nearly claimed his life and made him a triple amputee. He wears three prosthetics, quite proudly, and has served as a voice of advocacy for the disabled community. The résumé he built after his accident is incredibly impressive. After earning a degree in art history from Princeton, he then entered med school, subsequently becoming a physician. He currently works with patients who are nearing the end of their lives.

On the podcast he shared what exactly it is that makes him uniquely qualified to work with his patients. It's not his degrees or position in the community; it's not his theory on suffering or his knowledge of human anatomy. He explained, "Especially in my role in medicine, I find it's very useful, that my body and its obvious suffering is very useful. It's a means of building trust with people who are also suffering from their body failing in one way or another." BJ Miller can walk into a hospital room, where someone is lying on their death bed, suffering, the usefulness of their body fading, and immediately connect with them. They can plainly see he knows what it is like to lie in a hospital bed and face death, too.

In a 2011 article for *DailyGood,* Patricia Yollin wrote about Miller:

> He took premed courses in Denver and at Mills College in Oakland before starting medical school at UCSF in 1997, with the notion of entering rehabilitative medicine. He changed his mind after doing a rotation in that field.
>
> "I felt like a poster child," he said. "When I'd walk out of the room, I'd hear some family member say, 'See, he can do it!' And I knew what those guys needed was to wallow and get angry. They didn't need some jackass with really white teeth saying, 'Hey, you can climb a mountain!' They just wanted to learn how to take a leak again."

Inspiration on a grand scale is a glorious thing. It gives us a glimpse of the heights to which we can soar. It manifests hope to us and gives us a lofty goal to which we can aspire. It shows us the summit of the mountain and testifies, "See, you can do it, too!" But before you can climb a mountain, you have to be able to get out of your hospital bed. If there is anything of value I could hope to offer, it is this: I have lain in the same hospital bed as you. And while we all wear our dysfunction differently, we all wear it, nonetheless.

WHAT I WORE

I have been clinically diagnosed with anorexia nervosa. I have been less than 85 percent of my ideal body weight and as a result I had fine hair growing all over my face and arms to attempt to keep me warm because I had so little flesh to do so. The term for this is *lanugo.* I was also severely dehydrated. My bone density was affected and my digestive system was in a state of painful complete shutdown.

And beyond the physical manifestations, the obsessive-compulsive patterns of my thoughts were a torture unto themselves. Numbers and numbers and numbers—there were always numbers turning in my mind, in a revolving door of shame to which there was no ending. Patterns, routines, rituals—I was enslaved to them all. Food had to be cut into a certain number of pieces, a certain size. If I ate beyond a predetermined caloric limit, there was a self-imposed price to be paid. How many calories are in a postage stamp? Does anyone know? I had to know. How many calories are in a Tylenol? I had to know. Why doesn't anyone seem to know how many calories are in toothpaste?

And then there was the scale. The omnipotent judge, jury, and executioner. The scale was a callous and uncaring tyrant. Nothing else mattered.

I have also struggled with bulimia. I could only go so long without eating. When I could not stand the unbearable pain of hunger another minute, I would have to shamefully acquiesce and eat something forbidden. Sometimes once I started, I just couldn't stop. Visualizing the horrific outcome of my indiscretion, I would do the only thing I knew how to do to make it right. I had to purge to get rid of the food. Some days, I would purge up to ten times a day. I abused laxatives, taking handfuls at a time. My heart was constantly beating irregular rhythms. I was on the verge of blacking out daily. Some days I did. These were the days I felt the closest to death. Even now, it is almost too painful to describe the complete and total darkness of bulimia.

As surely as the eating disorder escalated, my ravening desire to be free of it escalated, too. Sometimes I could conjure enough willpower to stop the out-of-control behaviors for a few days, a few weeks, a few months. But even if I wasn't acting out severely in my eating disorder, my eating was always disordered. I would never, *ever* ask for help. Asking for help was a one-way ticket to being treated like a carnival sideshow or, worse, an object of pity. Pity was worse than death to me. Even if I were dying, I would be dying as the master of my own destiny, not as someone's sad, failed project. Plus, I needed the cover of secrecy. If I told someone, they might force me to stop. And as nightmarish as the eating disorder was, it was always there for me. I knew what it would give me. It was a soft place to land, even if that place was in the pit of hell.

I was able to break out of the deadly cycle of the eating disorder once in a while. But I always seemed to replace one damaging behavior with another. I went through a period of time when shopping and buying things helped me feel better; the problem with that particular diversion was the lack of funding. I would use surreptitiously obtained credit cards and then hide what I was doing from my husband. I could only conceal it for so long. My covert activities would soon be exposed in a shattering explosion of ruined trust, and I would have to face what I had done. We would attempt to fix the damage, but the devastation grew beyond repair.

I moved on to the next activity or cause. I became vegan, exercised like a maniac, had baby after baby after baby after baby. I tried going back to school (to become a therapist so I could help others, of course!). I hawked a line of all-natural makeup to my friends and family, redecorated my house, isolated, got involved, got uninvolved. I would buy a scale and then break it. And then buy another scale and then break that one. I desperately wanted to move away and start over—anywhere, just not here. I was always searching aimlessly, feeling depressed, blaming my husband for not being there for me, holding a grudge against my friends for not caring enough about me, and blaming God for not taking all of this away from me. And always, when none of that worked, I would return to the eating disorder, my insidiously loyal companion. Losing weight was something I could do. And I was darn good at it.

Losing weight demonstrated to others that I really *was* good at something.

A WAY THAT SEEMS RIGHT

Maybe, right now, you are thinking, *That is not me. I don't starve. I'm not dangerously underweight. In fact, I am the opposite—I feel as though I am addicted to food. I have carried extra weight as long as I can remember.* Maybe you couldn't begin to list the number of names you have been called, the complete self-loathing, the toll it has taken on your health and the quality of your life. Maybe you're afraid of food because you can't stop eating it.

I have heard many, many women share their own dark struggles with food. I have been in numerous support groups that included women with struggles in both extremes on the spectrum of food issues. Honestly, early on in my recovery, when a support group contained women who were both underweight and overweight, it usually ended up with them becoming adversaries. Neither side could understand or empathize with the other. One side would say, "It must be nice to be so thin." And the other side would say, "Just stop eating."

Though each side used food very differently, both had the same deep rooted belief about food: **We were convinced food that was powerful.** Eat the right amount of food. Eat the right type of food. That was the key to happiness. That was the key to being normal. According to that logic, if starting to eat food was the solution to the undereater's distress, then food would cure their eating disorder. If stopping food intake was the solution to the overeater's affliction, then not eating would lead to fulfillment. Food would resolve all misery. In its presence or its absence, food would be the keeper of the keys, the panacea to all heartache. Food would possess the power to fundamentally change who we are. Every diet plan has always promised this, after all. Every meal plan has put a 100 percent guarantee on that incontrovertible truth.

What if I told you a new truth?

What if I told you **it is not about food?**

Ask yourself this question: "Could I be happy if I never lost another pound or could never alter my physical appearance in any way?"

Paul wrote in Philippians 4:11, "I have learned to be content in whatever circumstances I am." Is that kind of a life possible or even imaginable for you right now? Do you long for that fulfillment? Do you long for an identity that has nothing to do with what you weigh? A purpose in life that is completely independent of what you put in your mouth to eat? Where successes and failures aren't measured against the tyranny of the scale? Where confidence isn't a slave to a size?

Perhaps you are reading this and thinking, *I know I have some issues, but I am really not that bad. My relationship with food is not ideal, it's not what I want it to be, but it is definitely not nearly as bad as what I have just read about.*

I have noticed that after someone in recovery shares a particularly powerful testimony filled with dramatic life-and-death events and miraculous restoration, those who have just listened to it say, *"Well, I might have some problems, but mine are nothing compared to what I have just heard. I really need to learn to keep my issues in perspective. I really don't have it that bad after all."*

I feel the urge to grab them (lovingly) and say, "Yes, they have had significant problems. Yes, their life was the train wreck of all train wrecks. Guess what? There is always someone who struggles more than you. There is always someone who has had more to overcome. Always! What does that have to do with you? Do *you* want a life that is free from "every weight and the sin that so easily ensnares us"? Do *you* want to be happy?"

DO YOU WANT TO GET WELL?

Comparison is the root of all unhappiness, food related or not. Do not ask yourself the question, "Am I sick enough?" but rather, "Do I want to get well?" In the gospel of John, chapter 5 we read an eyewitness account of an encounter between Jesus and a man who had been sick and disabled for thirty-eight years. Jesus made His way through a crowd congregated around a pool of water. These masses were patiently waiting, watching for the moment when, according to tradition, the angel would touch the water. When the waters were stirred, the first person able to enter the water would be healed. This crowd was filled with all manner of sick people: the blind, the lame, the paralyzed. They were gathered there for one purpose: they had a problem and they needed a miracle.

Jesus navigated the crowd and found His way to the man who had been an invalid for almost four decades. When He saw him, He had compassion on him because He "knew he had already been there a long time" and was in need of healing. Jesus didn't select this man based on any criteria or comparative analysis—He approached him because He saw that the man was suffering, alone, and He wanted him to be made whole. The Messiah stood before this man who was lying on the sickbed of his despair and pain and proceeded to ask him a question that seemed to defy logic. "Do you want to get well?"

Did he want to get well? What kind of a question was that? Of course he wanted to get well! The sick man had been suffering in that condition for an unquestionably long time. He had been lying day after day by a pool of water, helplessly waiting for the minuscule chance someone would wander by and help him get into the water before anyone else could. Chances are, he'd been waiting by that healing pool most of his life.

This question Jesus posed did seem to have an obvious answer. But I can unequivocally say from personal experience and much observation, yes is not always the ready and truthful answer. We hold on to our painful way of coping, and soldier on in our suffering, sickness, and dysfunction for so many reasons. It can be extraordinarily painful to lay it down, just like that. There is comfort in the familiar, even if it is a crippling familiarity. And an eating disorder is a familiar way of life. One of the most commonly reported ways people say they struggle with food is that they use food for comfort and solace. Honestly, who wants to lay down the only comfort they have ever known? That is heartrendingly difficult.

It may be that we feel we don't deserve forgiveness, let alone healing. We believe that we deserve our condition because we are responsible for it. Or perhaps we are mortified that if we reach out and say, "Yes! I want to get well," we will attempt to get up and everyone will see us fall on our faces. We steady our resolve to embrace this reality: **We have indeed made our beds, and now we resign ourselves to lie in them.**

Maybe some of these same rationalizations were turning in the sick man's mind at the pool of Bethesda. Jesus had asked him a ridiculous, brutally honest, soul-searching question, "Do you want to get well?" His response to Jesus indicated he had been living with his own litany of excuses. "I don't have a man to put me into the pool when the water is stirred up, but while I am coming, someone goes down ahead of me," he said. This man, who had been sick for thirty-eight long years, started to offer his own justifications of why he, ashamed and lying in the dirt, had not moved any closer to his healing. Jesus simply ignored him. The man needed no justification: Jesus was his justification.

"'Get up,' Jesus told him, 'pick up your bedroll and walk!'"

That is what I want you to know.

Whatever your past, whatever mistakes you have made . . .

Whatever has been done to you when you were innocent and defenseless . . .

However many times you have starved, binged, made yourself throw up, abused laxatives, lied, manipulated, rejected help, isolated yourself in shame, or chosen your eating disorder over those that love you . . .

It doesn't matter what you weigh or why you weigh that much . . .

It doesn't matter if you have treated your body in the most egregious ways possible . . .

It doesn't matter if you have tried and failed spectacularly one thousand times before . . .

Jesus is your justification.

He sees you right now, and He says, "Pick up your bedroll mat and walk." Sitting on the ground, staring into the eyes of the Savior, this man, lame, hopeless, deserted, and despairing, somehow believed after nearly forty years of being imprisoned by his body that change was possible.

Will you dare to believe with me?

CHAPTER 4

a Different Perspective

Each time I see the Upside-Down Man
Standing in the water,
I look at him and start to laugh,
Although I shouldn't oughtter.
For maybe in another world
Another time
Another town,
Maybe HE is right side up
And I am upside down.

"REFLECTION," SHEL SILVERSTEIN

When I was in treatment, we were required to attend a variety of classes. By "require," I mean we had to show up or else we were punished with a variety of consequences: loss of the privilege to go out with my family during family week, not being allowed to walk to class anymore but having to be driven around in a "people mover," getting a special room to sleep in at night so I could be watched twenty-four hours a day.

By "attend," I mean that I would sit, physically present in my seat, but with an expression full of loathing and venomous hatred. Or, I would sit in my chair and devote every minute to drawing as many minuscule stars on my paper as I could in forty-five minutes. I preferred outright insolence to being erroneously perceived as wanting to be there.

While in class, however, the tantalizing possibility always existed that someone would start to argue with the teacher. An event of this persuasion was, to me, an acceptable use of class time, and it was one of the only ways to rouse me from my militant disdain. It always struck me as funny in a way that was sadly ironic because we were all fully-grown women engaging in these antics. I remember one occasion when we spent an entire nutrition didactic class in a heated argument over the information we received which stated that white bread and wheat bread were really the same thing; one just had a brown color. This type of classroom diversionary brilliance became the standard to which we all aspired. We discussed this feat for days to come, *"I mean, who do they think they're fooling? It's a **fact** that wheat bread is made from wheat flour that has not been processed and bleached and enriched. Did you see how the teacher had nothing say in response to that?"*

In the next class, the teacher gave us a (beautiful) story by Max Lucado to read. *You Are Special* was about a village filled with Wemmicks, "people" who were made of wood and resembled spindly, marionette puppets. It was a story designed to enable us to see that God made us uniquely special with purpose, and that our value was not dependent on what others thought of us.

As the discussion time began, the teacher posed a question to us all. "By what standard did the Wemmicks judge value? How did they determine who received a star [a display of praise] and who received a dot [a show of criticism]?"

His eyes shone with expectant hope, the kind of hope and compassionate zeal that one either aspires to or condescends to. He anticipated that one of us was going to, in that very moment, begin to have a breakthrough. However, his eager optimism collided with the ugly reality of minds in the grip of an eating disorder.

"I thought the main character looked anorexic," someone said with a hollow look in her eyes.

"They aren't real, you know. They are fictional beings. The point is not about what they look like," the teacher stammered, trying to redirect the discussion.

I preyed on these kinds of moments. "Why would you show us pictures in a story of people—I'm sorry, 'fictional beings'—that are so thin? Are you trying to trigger us?" I said. The class was lost at that point and the teacher knew it. I felt deeply satisfied. To me, my whole experience in treatment was a complete and total waste of my time and I was determined to prove it.

Yet, despite my grim determination to undermine the entire process, there was one class that was the exception: the body image class. This class was taught by a young woman with shiny black hair and very fashionable clothes. She would show up in an outfit straight off the runway—high heels and a jaunty fedora. She walked with confidence and grace and always seemed happy. That was a mystery to me. To someone who judged life by control and weights and measures, it was a wholly remarkable thing. She just was. She was full of life, a beautiful butterfly that had landed from some faraway land. I wrote off her good cheer as an act that she was required to put on for our benefit. The treatment center was in the desert and begged for dusty practicality. As patients, we went around dressed in sweats and pajamas; the effort to comb our own hair was usually too much to ask. Yet, there she was, genial and well-groomed.

I wasn't alone in my evaluation of her. The vast majority of us felt the same way. As a result, when we were in her class, we listened and tried to understand what she was teaching us. She would tell us things like *"The idea that women are supposed to be thin is a very recent phenomenon. Throughout history this was not the case. Being thin or desiring to be thin is a thoroughly modern notion. It only is important now because we say it is important. If we, as women, decided that it was ridiculous and stopped believing it, we could change society."* Or,

"What does society say an ideal woman is? She needs to be thin and attractive. Sexy and sexual, but not too much so, because we have other names for that kind of a woman. She needs to have a brilliant, full-time career and have well-adjusted children with whom she spends all of her time. And on and on and on. But no one can possibly be all of those things. How could one person possibly be all of those things?" And finally, and maybe most importantly, *"Why are you valuable? Why do you matter? Do you matter because of anything you have done or said? No, you have value because you are created in the image of God. When He breathed life into you, He placed value in you that cannot be added to by any human effort. And it cannot be taken away from, either."*

Value.

The idea that I have value. And why I have value. I had never thought about it before. I had just mechanically believed what I had been telling myself for all those years. I believed that if I had enough willpower to change myself into the person I wanted to be, into the image I wanted to present the world, then I would be happy and fulfilled. But sitting there in a body image class in a treatment center, in a room that smelled like unwashed feet, I was neither happy nor fulfilled. This radical new idea of value began to take root in my soul.

ETERNAL PERSPECTIVE

Nate Saint, missionary to the Waodani people in the Amazonian region of Ecuador, wrote:

People who do not know the Lord ask why in the world we waste our lives as missionaries. They forget that they too are expending their lives . . . and when the bubble has burst, they will have nothing of eternal significance to show for the years they have wasted. . . . If God would grant us the vision, the word "sacrifice" would disappear from our lips and thoughts;

we would hate the things that seem now so dear to us; our lives would suddenly be too short; we would despise time-robbing distractions and charge the enemy with all our energies in the name of Christ.

If you consider that Nate Saint, along with four other young men, including Jim Elliot, were murdered for the cause of sharing the gospel, that statement takes on a significance beyond words. What kind of a young man would move to the jungle, far from the former comforts of his previous life, all for the sake of making contact with a tribe of people who had never before been engaged by outsiders? What sort of altruism would motivate someone to do this? What kind of human being prays for the vision to redefine *sacrifice?*

The answer is this: one who lives with eternal purpose. There is no other way to truly look beyond the temporal, the here and now, what we can see with our eyes, unless you are eternal. And there is no other way to have eternal life, except through Jesus Christ. Jesus said, "I am the way, the truth, and the life. No one comes to the Father except through Me" (John 14:6). John 3:36 says, "The one who believes in the Son has eternal life . . ."

Eternal perspective changes everything. It changed everything for those five missionaries. It changed everything for Jim Elliot's widow, Elisabeth, who, her young daughter left fatherless, was still able to say, "Of one thing I am perfectly sure: God's story never ends in 'ashes.'"

By all normal reckonings, the violent murder of her husband in the very prime of his life was an unspeakable tragedy. Without eternal perspective, there is no way this grievous calamity could be viewed as anything other than misfortune and failure. Yet, not only is it not viewed as failure by those most closely involved, on the contrary, it is viewed as a triumph. Certainly there is more than enough grief and pain to go around in their martyrdom. I'm sure these young missionaries talked about the possibility of death before they ventured into the jungle, but its shocking reality still brought heartbreaking sorrow, regardless of how willing they were to accept it. This statement, which Jim Elliot is synonymous with, brings all of that expectant sorrow into glorious clarity: "He is no fool who gives what he cannot keep to gain which he cannot lose."

Eternal perspective really does change everything. With it, value has a prime meridian by which it can now be judged. Eternity provides the latitude and longitude by which value can be charted. In the light of eternity, value is, and it is whatever God says it is. And He said, "Now you are no longer a slave, but God's own child. And since you are his child, God has made you his heir" (Galatians 4:7, nlt). The value He placed in you is value that makes you His own child, both now and for all eternity. Embracing eternal perspective is nothing more than recognizing that the value God has placed in you is more meaningful than anything this world has to offer.

Conversely, it would follow to reason, without eternal perspective, the pursuit of being thin and controlling your weight at any cost is indeed a lofty goal. The temporal world values being thin. The nonenduring world values outward appearances. It might say it doesn't, but please—that is an outrageous hypocritical platitude. The reality is exactly the opposite. The $66.3 billion diet industry tells us that what matters most is *not* what is on the inside (Marketplace Data, Inc.).

Even our families often reinforce that same message. One woman shared with me, "When, I was in junior high, my mother told my dad that I was getting pudgy. I was devastated, as I was always taught to look at someone's heart, not their appearance. It changed my whole worldview." Scroll through Facebook or Instagram and you will see how very happy people can be when they are in control of their weight. They have the selfies to prove it! They have the before and after shots! And they are dying to help you participate in their latest dietary revelation. And why not? If you are not eternal, this physical body is a means to an end unto itself. Your philosophical view of what the physical body is then determines body image. And that body image, which is based upon the physical body, in turn, determines what you believe about self-worth.

Throughout my pursuit of recovery, I was terrified of what the future would look like if I truly let go of my weight. I was certain it would mean I would have to let myself go, physically speaking. And that, to me, was a depressing outcome. But there was one hoped-for outcome that did not depress me out of my mind. If this *one thing* would happen, then I would know I was finally free. I would know that I was finally recovered when I would, once and for all, have a positive body image. I would love and appreciate my body for what it was, exactly how it was.

I want to pause and say it is absolutely possible to have a positive body image. It is extremely healthy to honestly see my body for what it is, and what it is not, and to still be grateful for the gift of my body. Our bodies are indeed fearfully and wonderfully made vehicles that allow us to live a life full of meaning and joy. A restored body image is a noble standard to aspire to. That kind of body image exchanges a life ruled by shame for a life governed by thankfulness. It truly is a blessing to wake up in the morning and recognize my body is a miracle, beautifully designed and graciously bestowed by God. It is a magnificent goal to aim for in recovery.

Even though a healthy, positive body image is a wonderful goal, if we stop there, we miss out on something even more life changing. At the end of the day, a well-adjusted body image is still dependent on something temporary. Positive body image is dependent upon our bodies.

Sir Isaac Newton said:

I don't know what I may seem to the world, but as to myself, I
seem to have been only like a boy playing on the sea-shore and
diverting myself in now and then finding a smoother pebble or a
prettier shell than ordinary, whilst the great ocean of truth lay all
undiscovered before me.

Eternal perspective is the "great ocean of truth." It revolutionizes
my view of my body, whether my body be worthy of appreciation
or not, whether it be functioning beautifully or not, whether I find
my body to be useful, or whether I find myself trapped in a useless
one. Eternal perspective colors my body's traitorous state of being,
all my thoughts, all my struggles, all my vast insufficiencies, all my
dreams and deepest desires, with real and living hope. And hope
does not disappoint.

I AM ETERNAL

God created me, body and soul.

William Walsham wrote:

What a wonderful thing the soul is . . . You cannot see it: you
cannot hear it: you cannot touch it. Yet you know it is there. You
do not want any proof that you have a soul. You are as sure of
that as that you have a body. It tells you itself.

Now, I think I am wrong, after all, in saying that you have a
soul. Ought I not to say, you are a soul? . . . In truth . . . it is the
soul that has a body, not the body that has a soul; for the soul is
greater surely than the body, and will last when the body is laid
aside in death.

As a believer in Jesus Christ, my soul is eternal. Therefore, I am
eternal. *"We are not human beings having a spiritual experience. We*

are spiritual beings having a human experience" (Pierre Teilhard de Chardin). This a liberating truth; it transforms all things. It is the light by which I am able see the way to lasting freedom. In this light, I am able to accurately see that my physical body is not all there is of me. God created my body, and it is good, but it is a means to an end. This world as I am experiencing it now is temporary, and my body is temporary. I am eternal!

This belief was fundamental to me in recovery from my eating disorder. I remember the first moment I realized I truly believed I was an eternal soul having a brief physical experience. I literally shouted out, *"Take that, eating disorder! All I have to do is put up with this body for a little while longer! I am eternal!"* I was standing at the kitchen sink washing the dishes at the time of my triumphant proclamation, so my children were somewhat alarmed and started moving out of the kitchen at a rapid pace.

My children's reaction notwithstanding, I knew at that moment I was on the path of a serious plan of action to conquer my eating disorder once and for all. It is a simple thought, I know. Yet, this thought—that my body, as I am experiencing it now, is temporary—has broken serious thought patterns and areas of bondage in my life.

So what if my pants don't fit like they used to? I am eternal. Who cares if I haven't seen the inside of a gym for years? I am eternal. I tried a new food for the simple enjoyment of it, and I liked it. I am eternal. What does it matter that I have a giant pimple on my face? I am eternal. Why should I care what size the label in my clothes says? I am eternal. Let old age and wrinkles come. I am eternal. Yes, I've made mistakes. I am eternal. There is now no condemnation for those who are in Christ Jesus. I am eternal.

I want to take a moment to offer clarification to the whole notion that our bodies are simply physical things with which we must contend in the here and now until we can "get through" to the other side. I am not trying to revive Gnosticism. Gnosticism is the belief that physical matter and the human body are inherently evil, that human beings are actually spirits, trapped in physical bodies from which we must escape. This view determines that the temporary world, all that we see with our eyes now and experience in the physical realm, is something that must be transcended. It renders the experience of flesh and bone that we are having now as meaningless, as something that has no bearing whatsoever on who we are as spiritual beings because it is by its nature, evil. Spirit is good. Physical is bad.

The knowledge that we are eternal, in light of the incarnation and resurrection of Christ, is so much greater than the narrow definition of the Gnostics. If we are believers in Jesus Christ, the eternal is now. The fact that we are eternal, right now, does not negate the role and the influence of the physical realm. Rather, it informs it. The incarnation and Resurrection transform the *now* we currently live in. Everything that composes life for us in the here and now has been forever changed and given meaning by the Cross. The Cross was a moment in time that covers all moments in time. Although what we are experiencing right now in the physical world is temporary, it is not meaningless. The psalmist wrote, "I would have lost heart, unless I had believed that I would see the goodness of the Lord in the land of the living" (Psalm 27:13, nkjv).

Therefore, the sentiment that my physical body is something temporary that must be managed until I am able to get through to the other side is not a depressing paradox that pits the spirit world against the physical one. Honestly, for me, it is a worldview that was a very helpful tool in breaking free from the eating disorder. I felt I was imprisoned in a body over which I had no control. Until that dysfunctional cycle of thought could be broken, it was enormously helpful for me to forget about my body altogether.

Viewing my body as something I merely had to contend with for just a little while longer, in the same way a paraplegic would contend with their noncompliant body, freed me from the burden of needing to control it. It was a temporary measure, viewing my body in that way—a stand-in-the-gap intervention which got me through to a place where I was healthy enough to start making properly informed decisions concerning my body and its usefulness. It was a tool, used and considered in the light of eternal perspective.

My body isn't useless at all. That is the truth. Whether it is functioning properly or not, it is useful. I will go into much greater detail about this in the chapters to come, but for now, I wanted to lay a solid foundation: "For no one can lay any other foundation than what has been laid down. That foundation is Jesus Christ" (1 Corinthians 3:11). Seeing Christ for who He is, *is* eternal perspective.

For our momentary light affliction is producing for us an absolutely incomparable eternal weight of glory. So we do not focus on what is seen, but on what is unseen; for what is seen is temporary, but what is unseen is eternal.
2 Corinthians 4:17-18

Viewing life through this lens changes everything. Outward circumstances beyond our control may not change, but our reactions and the way we respond to circumstances do change. We are able to look at whatever used to cause us intense fear and agony and decide to view it as temporary. We have the strength to get through anything, because we are eternal.

Your struggle is unique. I would never presume to hand out universal advice and consider it law. Every person has arrived at the point of their extreme pain by a completely different road. Suffering is relative, but the fact that it is relative is completely irrelevant. The question that needs to be answered is the same, though: Do you want to get well? For me, I could only answer it when I got brutally honest. I had to admit that while I was a believer in Jesus Christ, I had placed my own beliefs about what really mattered in life above what God said really mattered. I wasn't obsessed with controlling food and my weight because of extreme vanity, which is a very widely held belief about people who struggle with eating disorders. I was obsessed with trying to prove to myself that I had purpose, that I mattered to God and to others. I put my own way of proving that I mattered above God, who had already proved I matter.

A very ugly reality I needed to face about myself was that I had believed, despite my Christian faith, that I was a body first and foremost, and not a soul. I realized that I alone had the power to make the decision to confront the ugly lie and believe the truth. The new reality I needed to embrace is that I am a soul. Once I decided I could seize this new reality, standing upon the everlasting love of the risen Savior, I began to do so, one thought at a time. Because, as Elisabeth Elliot so beautifully wrote, "Heaven is not here, it's There. If we were given all we wanted here, our hearts would settle for this world rather than the next. God is forever luring us up and away from this one, wooing us to Himself and His still invisible Kingdom where we will certainly find what we so keenly long for."

I am eternal.

CHAPTER 5

The Root of the Problem

Who will rescue me from this body of death?
ROMANS 7:24

My battle with bulimia began in earnest when I was a sophomore in college. The first two years of college I played volleyball on a scholarship. Going from high school to college was definitely a culture shock for me as far as the advanced ability of the players, the level, and the speed of the game. As I was adjusting to playing a sport on the college level, I was also adjusting to the fact that I could not let myself eat.

I had begun severely restricting my food intake at the end of my senior year in high school. Everything I had ever known about my life until that time was undergoing dramatic change; high school was coming to an end and I was preparing to attend a college nineteen hours away from home. Every activity I enjoyed during my years in high school was drawing to a close as well; there would be no going back.

I was a very high achiever. The quintessential perfectionist. I was a very good girl who, in spite of her put-together appearance, carried dark secrets, one of which was a sexual assault that happened when I was fourteen years old. I never told anyone. I worked maniacally throughout the intervening teenage years to erase from my mind what could never be erased—that I was really not a good girl. I was damaged, and I ought to be ashamed.

I worked as hard as I could, incessantly striving, participating in every activity that came my way. I was desperately trying to convince others that I really was good. I could prove it—see! I had done all of these impressive things. Yet, as high school wound its way down, impressive achieving was harder to come by. I was weary, worn ragged from the relentless pursuit of excellence, from constantly trying to not think about myself...what I really thought about myself.

I needed a new cure for the problem of my shame.

I don't know where I got the idea to start skipping meals. One day at lunch as I sat there surveying the activity in the room, I became conscious that everyone else was eating and I was not. I was abruptly aware of the sounds of chewing and the greedy way people were shoving food into their faces. It was revolting to me. I looked down at the unopened lunch bag in my lap, and I felt powerful in a way I never had before.

From that moment on, I basically stopped eating and hunger became the new cure for my shame. At first, it was lovely; this remedy for my guilt delivered all that it promised. I felt proud as I lost weight. People noticed and were impressed. It was also such a relief to have a routine on which I could depend. The same food, cut up in the same way, followed by the same sets of exercises. I could fall asleep at night, painfully hungry, knowing that in the morning I would wake up weighing less.

This pattern of restricting food and weight loss continued into the first year of college. Anorexia was my new friend. It helped me forget the things I needed to forget and to have the confidence to face a new overwhelming life. Anorexia became dear to me; it held the place of highest preeminence in my life. I soon began to realize it was affecting my ability to play volleyball on the level I needed to, but I also realized that I needed the eating disorder to make it through the day. Forget one day at a time—I needed it to face one meal at a time.

Besides that, my coach was very thin, and I was irrationally convinced that she had an eating disorder as well. The fact that she noticed how little I was eating and tried to coerce me to eat was just proof to me that she was petty and manipulative and on a power trip. Who did she think she was trying to tell me what to do concerning my eating disorder? Yet despite all this, and in spite of my waning physical stamina, I managed to perform well enough to earn a position on the varsity team. I even earned the Most Improved Player and the Freshman of the Year awards. My grades were still straight A's. If I disregarded the constant mental anguish I was in, I saw no rational reason to change anything I was doing.

My shame remained safely hidden away . . . until the fall of my sophomore year. The strained relationship I had with my coach continued to deteriorate. She had placed the entire team on a very strict nutritional program—and she meant business. Looking back, I see that it was an entirely reasonable thing for a college coach to do. Food was fuel, after all. In theory, the quality of our performance would reflect the quality of our nutritional intake. A list of acceptable and unacceptable foods was presented. There were to be no deviations from this list, or else there would be consequences. If there was to be any indulging, it would occur because the coach permitted it. I deeply resented her for deigning to interfere in the way I was allowed to use food, which I considered to be sacred.

From time to time, she would call me into her office to express her concern over my apparent eating disorder. I felt humiliated and enraged by her hypocrisy. At one point I openly accused her of having an eating disorder, too. She responded by arranging visits to doctors for me, and eventually began to make vague threats that I would not be awarded my scholarship for the next year if things did not change. There are no words to describe how much I loathed her. I realize in hindsight that it was not her, but rather the way I reacted to her that ruined all hope. It became the perfect storm. Under other circumstances things could have worked out so differently, but I was not prepared to face life without my eating disorder. The eating disorder tainted everything with tragedy.

My relationship with my coach and my own horrible coping strategy turned disastrous.

I decided I would show her who the real boss was. I said hateful things about her behind her back. I defied her to her face. I didn't care if I never played again; I just wanted her to suffer. But the ultimate display of my disdain for her was that I started to sneak and eat all the things we were forbidden to eat. Things I would have never eaten if I had been left to my own devices. I ordered those types of food at restaurants when we were on the road for games and relished the power struggle that ensued when she tried to tell me no. I was determined to best her at every turn, no matter what the cost.

The volleyball season ended, and I quit the team. I had loved playing volleyball so much, and I gave it up without a second thought, all for the sake of an eating disorder. I would never play college volleyball again. The sad reality was that I didn't mourn this loss for what it really was; I was in mourning for other reasons. All of the calorie-rich junk food I had been eating in an act of defiance had taken a toll on me. I was gaining weight, and that was completely and totally unacceptable. Panic consumed me; I didn't know what to do. It didn't seem as easy as it was before to be hungry all the time because I had become used to eating, and now it was hard to stop. Then, in a sad, sad moment of desperation, the solution came to me: all I had to do was get rid of the food.

The decision I made to begin purging was tantamount to deciding to throw myself into the abyss of hell. I wanted to die. I fantasized about dying day and night. It was so hard to be sneaky with bingeing and purging at college because I lived in a dorm. Someone was always around. To avoid watchful, prying eyes, I would drive off campus and stay there as long as I could. I prowled the campus looking for unused classrooms and bathrooms. I was living in a nightmare, but I could not stop what I was doing.

Attending classes became secondary to my eating disorder. I knew I was squandering opportunity after opportunity, but regret was a luxury I couldn't afford to have. I shoved regret down into the darkness of the eating disorder, where it could be swallowed up, just like shame and guilt had been. No one knew what I was up to. Every ounce of my energy and resolve that were not being used up by bulimia were used to appear perfect. Appearing perfect was the only defense I possessed against the ravages of my suffering.

At one point, someone outright asked me if I had an eating disorder. The residence hall director called me into her office. She asked me if I had been making myself throw up, because someone had reported to her that I had been seen entering the bathroom directly after every meal time.

I looked her right in the eye and lied. "No, I have not."

She looked back at me, and I knew that she knew I was lying. "Are you sure . . . ? I mean, you can tell me anything. Well, if you don't want to admit it . . . you can get help . . . ," she bleated lamely. But what could she do about it? I certainly didn't care what she thought. Everyone else thought I had it all. I had achieved what my physical self wanted from me: to be very thin and to appear to have it all together.

My drive to appear as though I had it all together led me to do some very unusual things. I could not bear the thought of anyone seeing me take out the trash. As in, empty the trash can and take the garbage bag full of trash outside to the Dumpster. I can offer no explanation other than I would be filled with humiliation if anyone saw me holding a bag of garbage. Trash was dirty and shameful. It smelled and it was a collection of all the things that had absolutely no use to anyone. I would stuff discarded papers in an unused suitcase, which I kept in the closet. Actual garbage was trickier. Not only did I have to hide the fact that I had it, but I was forced to try to find a way to dispose of it under stealth. I had a roommate and a suitemate, who were both part of the solution and part of the problem. At times, they would go ahead and take out the trash, so my dilemma was thus resolved. But other times, I was forced to get up at four in the morning to sneak out and throw it in the Dumpster, when I was sure no one was looking.

In a stroke of pure coincidence, both my roommate and suitemate decided to not return to school that following semester. This was a dream come true for me. I no longer had to sneak around campus like some disturbed nighttime prowler. This also meant that there was a whole adjoining room available for me to keep my trash in so that I would not have to take it out in public. I could place it in there and shut the door on the shameful congregation of trash. As the bags began to pile up, I realized with mounting concern that this was not sustainable. I had garbage that was in need of disposal. But I kept putting it in there, pretending that the day would never come when someone would discover what I was doing.

One day it happened. The very same residence hall director who had confronted me about my eating disorder burst into my room while I was in bed, trying to sleep. Her form was silhouetted against the light in the hallway.

"Why in the world is the room next door filled with garbage?" she demanded. To me, her appearance was that of a judge who had come to condemn me and my trash.

I lay there, not daring to look at her again. What could I possibly say in my defense? I had put the trash there. I had hidden it and I was ashamed of it. I could not face it.

I began to weep. She looked at me with an expression that re-sembled pity and shut my door. She cleaned the garbage out of the room the next day, and not another word was ever spoken about it.

The room full of bags of trash represented everything that was wrong with me. I felt so alone. I couldn't face all that garbage: the hurt and the loathing and the despair and the ugly secrets. I just kept shoving it into a place where I didn't have to look at it. But I knew it was there. And I knew it was not just bags of real garbage that could simply be taken to the Dumpster and disposed of. It was me. I had let all of my rotting shame and pain and deception pile up inside me. At any moment, someone could burst in and discover that I was not what I appeared to be. And then what would I do? **What could I do to defend myself against me?**

THE STRUGGLE IS REAL

For we know that the law is spiritual, but I am made out of flesh, sold into sin's power. For I do not understand what I am doing, because I do not practice what I want to do, but I do what I hate. And if I do what I do not want to do, I agree with the law that it is good. So now I am no longer the one doing it, but it is sin living in me. For I know that nothing good lives in me, that is, in my flesh. For the desire to do what is good is with me, but there is no ability to do it. For I do not do the good that I want to do, but I practice the evil that I do not want to do. Now if I do what I do not want, I am no longer the one doing it, but it is the sin that lives in me. So I discover this principle: when I want to do good, evil is with me. For in my inner self I joyfully agree with God's law. But I see a different law in parts of my body, waging war against the law of my mind and taking me prisoner to the law of sin in the parts of my body. What a wretched man

I am! Who will rescue me from this body of death? I thank God
through Jesus Christ our Lord!
Romans 7:14-25

There really could be no better way to describe what was going
on inside me as I grappled to survive in treatment. Twelve years had
passed between the moment the door flung wide-open, exposing
my piles of trash, and the day I entered the inpatient treatment
center. Twelve years of falling and getting up, struggling and suc-
ceeding, failing and failing and failing again. Twelve years of using
dieting, disordered eating, starvation, and bingeing and purging to
cover the condition of my guilt and shame. Twelve years of suffocating under the weight of knowing I was trapped in a cycle of
wretched behavior. Twelve years of attempting to keep the secret of
who I really was from everyone, but above all, from myself.

The problem was *me*. How could I possibly hope to be free of
me? I was a believer in Jesus Christ, and as such, the Spirit of God
lived inside me. But there was also a relentless, savage fight raging
within me, between the Spirit and what was contrary to the Spirit;
tension between the longing to be led by the Spirit into life, and
what the apostle Paul defines as the "flesh." **The flesh is the part of
me that is hostile to God, the part of me that is empty, seeking to fill itself and find its fulfillment apart from the love and
mercy and grace of Jesus.**

This battle between the Spirit and the flesh roared in me as I
struggled between using food the way God intended and using
food in a way God never intended. It manifested itself in unhealthy
and very self-destructive behaviors that were by-products of the lies
I believed. Lies about my value and worth, lies that I ought to be
ashamed, that I was guilty, that I was responsible for all the wrongs
that had happened to me. I believed the lie that if I could control
food, then I could control what was uncontrollable; I could control

myself, my circumstances, my past.

But there was one major failing in this plan. It was something fundamental I needed to learn in order to take the next step in my healing.

Food was not the problem.

DRAGON FLESH

God is the creator of food, after all.

> God also said, "'Look, I have given you every seed-bearing plant on the surface of the entire earth and every tree whose fruit contains seed. This food will be for you, for all the wildlife of the earth, for every bird of the sky, and for every creature that crawls on the earth—everything having the breath of life in it. I have given every green plant for food." And it was so. God saw all that He had made, and it was very good.
> Genesis 1:29-31

Food is a good gift that keeps on giving. It is fuel to nourish us and give us strength to do the work of His Kingdom, to celebrate life's joys with one another, and to fellowship together, as we share this experience of being flesh and bone.

Eating food is part of being alive. Its sustained presence is necessary to survive in this temporal world. The continued existence of food is perpetuated by ongoing natural cycles and processes which have been created by God as well; green leafy plants grow by photosynthesis, which in turn produce oxygen, which in turn support human and animal life on earth. Nature is a wonder, a beautiful, tenacious demonstration of creativity. It goes on, each moment a renewal of the original creation, in reflection of a good God's benevolence.

G. K. Chesterton described nature as "not our Mother; Nature is our sister. We can be proud of her beauty, since we have the same father; but she has no authority over us; we have to admire, but not to imitate. . . . Nature is a sister, and even a younger sister; a little, dancing sister, to be laughed at as well as loved."

Think about it. The same eternal perspective that informs our view of our physical bodies also informs our view of nature, of which food is a part. We human beings do not exist as spirit only and the earth as something else altogether different and alien. We are of the same stuff. God is the Father of it all. The difference lies in the fact that we are, to follow Chesterton's analogy, the older sibling. We are the elder sibling, and we have the birthright; we have been made in God's image, and nature, which includes food, has not. But that does not diminish the fact that we should see food, and its intended place and purpose in our lives, through the eyes of eternal perspective.

Eternal perspective tells us food was never intended to have preeminence over us. When we view food as powerful or addictive, we turn it into a controlled substance that is to be feared and avoided at all costs. You may protest, "But I'm addicted to _____. It's a scientific fact!"

To which I would simply say, "That is all fine and good, but do you want to get well? Do you want to be free?" I'm talking about fearless, audacious, joyful freedom. I'm talking about the kind of deliverance that is diametrically opposed to what my flesh desires. The flesh wants me to put food in categories, to eat it with guilt and reservation, to slink around afterward like a reprehensible rule breaker. The flesh wants me to believe the lie that I am addicted to food. The flesh wants me to find its nirvana in keeping my diet under control, under its boot. The flesh wants to dominate me and lead me to death. It wars against me unceasingly, trying to achieve this destructive end.

When I look back now at myself, a seventeen-year-old girl with an unopened lunch, I realize that I began to believe and embrace what my flesh proffered as a solution for controlling my shame. The solution it suggested seemed harmless enough. Skipping one meal was certainly nothing to be alarmed about. And so I listened and obeyed its first seemingly innocuous suggestion. But as days turned into weeks and months and years, the once innocent-natured requests of my flesh turned insidious, and on that dark day, when I stared in abject horror at the piles and piles of my trash, I knew I was no longer just coping: I was now enslaved. The path into slavery was a slow descent, but I arrived nonetheless. I hadn't even noticed it was happening. I had been simply putting one foot in front of the other, never perceiving that the sun was becoming obscured by thick and foreboding clouds. Too late I felt the weight of the shackles. I was now in chains and no longer had the strength to remove them by myself.

C. S. Lewis wrote about a miserable little boy in *The Voyage of the Dawn Treader:* "There was a boy called Eustace Clarence Scrubb, and he almost deserved it. . . . He didn't call his Father and Mother 'Father' and 'Mother,' but Harold and Alberta. They were very up-to-date and advanced people." Eustace, along with his cousins, Lucy and Edmund Pevensie, fell into an enchanted painting and found themselves on an adventure together in the magical land of Narnia. Sailing on a ship called the *Dawn Treader,* Eustace became caught up in a quest of which he wanted no part. He felt as though he was undeservedly singled out as an object of everyone's derision because of his superior station in life. When he and the crew landed on an unknown island, he sought out the first opportunity to sneak away and free himself of his loathsome shipmates.

He wandered too far and was forced to shelter in a mountainside cave that had previously been the domicile of dragon. As one could reasonably have expected, the dragon's lair was filled with bountiful treasure. Caught up in a moment of covetous wonder, he picked up a small golden hoop and slid it on his arm to wear as a bracelet for his upper arm. He fell asleep, exhausted, and when he woke up, "he had turned into a dragon. . . . Sleeping on a dragon's hoard with greedy, dragonish thoughts in his heart, he had become a dragon himself." While he slept, he was unaware that the dragon thoughts had taken over and were in the process of rendering him a prisoner of a monstrous new body. At first, he felt relief. "There was nothing to be afraid of any more. He was a terror himself now and nothing in the world . . . would dare to attack him." But this feeling of misplaced comfort soon turned into shock and grief at his new condition. He pitied himself, resigning himself to be trapped forever and all time as a beast of wrath.

But then something very strange happened to the dragon-Eustace. He described it like this:

> I looked up and saw the very last thing I expected: a huge lion coming slowly toward me. And . . . there was no moon . . . but there was moonlight where the lion was. So it came nearer and nearer. I was terribly afraid of it. You may think that, being a dragon, I could have knocked any lion out easily enough. But it wasn't that kind of fear. I wasn't afraid of it eating me. I was just afraid of *it*. . . . It came close up to me and looked straight into my eyes. And I shut my eyes tight. But that wasn't any good because it told me to follow it.

The lion led him to a garden filled with trees and fruit—and a well big enough to bathe in. And standing there, in the moonlight in the presence of such a fierce and awesome lion, dragon-Eustace knew he needed to take off his hard, thick, and scaly outer layer in order to be able to enter the water. He gave it his best effort, managing to remove a thin outer layer of his scales, much like a snake sheds its skin. But when he had done it, he looked down at himself, and he knew he had many, many, many layers that had to come off and he was incapable of doing it himself. He knew he needed the lion's help. So in spite of his fears, and because of his desperation, he laid down to let the mighty lion "undress" him.

The lion tore into him. Dragon-Eustace said:

> I thought it had gone right into my heart. . . . Well, he peeled the beastly stuff right off . . . and there it was lying on the grass: only ever so much thicker, and darker, and more knobbly-looking than the others had been. . . . And [he] threw me into the water . . . and as soon I started swimming and splashing I found that all the pain had gone . . . I'd turned into a boy again.

Thinking dragon thoughts had turned an unknowing Eustace into a dragon. He didn't set out to be trapped in the body of a ferocious, mythical creature, but he became trapped, even so. And once Eustace was dragonned, becoming un-dragonned was something he could not possibly accomplish himself. He could not will himself to become a boy again. He could not ignore his dragon self. He could not ask his friends for help, for there was nothing they could have done anyway, apart from comforting him through his sorrows. The only thing he could have done was take a leap of faith in the moonlight, following the lead of the King of the Beasts. Allowing the mighty lion to have his way with the scaly, hardened flesh-self, though it hurt ever so much, and though Eustace was greatly afraid.

One final word on Eustace Scrubb. Eustace could very well have lived out his days as a dragon. He wasn't worthless as a dragon. He was, after all, a living, breathing creature, alive and free on the face of the earth. And actually, he was still Eustace underneath that knobbly exterior. Eustace didn't remain a dragon for one reason, and one reason only: he wanted to return to his true self—the pale, incorrigible little boy that he always was, much loved by the Lion.

He wanted to change, to return to a place of wholesomeness, a place he wasn't sure even existed anymore, a place free from the tyranny of golden hoops and dragonish thoughts. The great Lion had simply been waiting, waiting, patiently waiting, for the moment Eustace himself was finally ready to submit to whatever the Lion wanted him to do. The Lion was his only hope.

> I say then, walk by the Spirit and you will not carry out the desire of the flesh. For the flesh desires what is against the Spirit, and the Spirit desires what is against the flesh; these are opposed to each other…
> Galatians 5:16-17

The flesh desires what is contrary to the Spirit. It is rebellious and hostile toward God. It seeks to go its own way. It is unrelenting and it is inescapable. It is all of that and so much more. It is truly a formidable foe.

But above and beyond all of that, it is one thing more: It is defeated.

CHAPTER 6

The Usurper

Batter my heart, three person'd God; for, you
As yet but knocke, breathe, shine, and seeke to mend;
That I may rise, and stand, o'erthrow mee', and bend
Your force, to breake, blowe, burn and make me new.
I, like an usurpt towne, to'another due . . .

SONNET XIV, JOHN DONNE

It was a travesty. Perhaps the greatest travesty in the long and sto-
ried history of Thanksgiving. I sat in the middle of a row of narrow
tables that had been pushed together, the customarily used round
tables set aside. We were celebrating togetherness. Our handmade
place mats were in front of us, in their newly laminated glory. We
had lovingly fashioned them out of construction paper and stickers
the weekend before as a part of our "craft experiential." There was
a festive array of pilgrim and pumpkin decorations, and since we
were not allowed to name or mention any specific food, we amused
ourselves with talking about the "stereotypical orange globe-shaped
gourd" centerpieces as often as we dared.

The actual Thanksgiving meal was on a cafeteria tray laden with
the old standbys. The portions were bigger than we were accustomed to, since this was an effort to normalize eating a largish meal
on a celebratory occasion. On that very day of giving thanks, I had

been in inpatient residential treatment at the eating disorder clinic for almost a whole month. A whole month had passed since I had seen my little girls. A month since I had been able to drive a car, walk freely out in the world, use a cell phone, or carry my purse. A month since I had been able to use scissors that were not chained to the table. A month since my husband had held me in his arms.

At the time I was in treatment, my husband, John, and I had been married for over eleven years. We met in college. To many people, we were an unlikely match—he, a toughened football player with a tumultuous upbringing and a zest for life, and me, a goody-two-shoes with a perfectly put together facade that masked sadness inside. I wouldn't say it was love at first sight—love requires so much more than merely beholding someone—but it was darn close. It was "knowing at first sight." I knew from the minute I was introduced to John that he was the one for me. We immediately became inseparable.

To John, life was an adventure to be seized and lived to the fullest. He brought out the wonder in me, wonder I long since believed had been robbed from me. That may seem like an unusual quality to prize in a romance, but to me, it was rapture. It was just what I needed. John was what I needed.

One evening, just before Thanksgiving break, we found ourselves in a used car lot. Well, it was more like a used car graveyard. I really and truly can't recall why we were there. That night, the snow was falling in white curtains, blanketing the rusty, broken-down shells of the decomposing cars, transforming them.

It seemed to me that we were standing on the grounds of a ramshackle manor house; the formal garden left long ago to go wild; the remnants of the days of glory could still be seen, soft forms rising from the earth like ancient ruins, white and gleaming in the moonlight. We were so close that I could see the snowflakes on

John's lashes. He kissed me for the first time in that snow covered garden-of-broken-down-vehicles.

Not long after that, he told me he loved me. I responded, "I love you as much as I can right now." Yes, I really said that.

Looking back, I can see that exchange embodied our entire relationship. It was true in the beginning and it remained true through the years that followed. John loved me, and I loved him. I loved him so much that I wanted to be completely honest with him. But I didn't know how to let him love me. I feared that if he knew me—really knew me—he would no longer love me. How could anyone?

John has made a lifelong habit of saving people. He is a social worker, a therapist, and a pastor who works with people in recovery. He is always busy, recklessly busy, ministering to others, helping to steer their lives away from the jagged rocks of disaster. His heart for the hurting is unparalleled. He leaves a trail of restored lives in his wake. Naturally, he wanted to save me, as well.

This was a lovely ideal, but it didn't make for the best foundation in a marriage. John's compulsive need to save me, combined with my "problems," resulted in a cycle of insanity: *I begged John to save me…he tried to save me……maybe I wasn't ready to be saved…maybe I didn't want to be saved….he couldn't save me…he got angry…I became contrite and vowed that I would change…I begged John to save me…*

His zeal to help the helpless appeared to finally have reached its limit. Thirteen years after our first kiss he told me he was done. "Get help, or we are through," he said. He simply could not understand why I was so hell-bent on self destruction when so many people were reaching out to offer me support. When he was moving heaven and earth to pluck me from ruin, time and time again.

I can never begin to imagine what he must have gone through, in trying to love and help a wife who just could not stop living a life dedicated to devastation. Throughout the course of our marriage, not only had I dealt with anorexia and bulimia, but depression was also a constant. Some days he would have to do it *all*—and I mean *all*. I am deeply thankful for everything he did for me during that dark time in our lives.

As I sat there at that Thanksgiving table, in the crucible of my new reality, I reached a breaking point. The feeding tubes didn't bother me anymore, and neither did the ever-present cafeteria food I was forced to eat. I was accustomed to waking up before dawn every day to be weighed, asking permission to use a Q-tip or dental floss, watching my packages being rifled through before I was allowed to have them. I had settled into being in treatment; there was a routine and a pattern and a rhythm.

What pushed me over the edge was the realization that I shouldn't have to be used to being in treatment. It was unfathomable that I—a mother and a wife with a home of her own—was enduring this mockery of a Thanksgiving. I should be pulling my own turkey out of my own oven. The delicious smells of spices and sweet things baking should be wafting through my own house. My own table, in my own dining room, should be filled with my own children, not with this disturbing array of dysfunction that filled the table before me. In that moment, the stalking beast of comprehension overtook me, and I decided I was done with it all. It was too hard and it was supremely unjust. I needed to talk to my husband. I should be allowed to at least talk to my husband, for the love of God, on the lowest day of my entire existence.

I began to sob uncontrollably. We hadn't even taken one nibble of the first course when I placed my face in my hands and started to weep and wail. This was not an unheard of experience at the dinner table, weeping and wailing, so everyone knew to discreetly look away.

The treatment worker stationed at my right elbow offered some encouraging instruction. "Now, I know this is hard, but you have to eat it. Finish this plate of food in half an hour, and it will all be over."

I couldn't even breathe at that point, let alone chew food and swallow it. Tears were pouring down like Niagara Falls into my turkey.

She offered further advice. "Take one bite and then I'm sure you will be able to take another bite, and before you know it, your whole plate will be empty!" Her voice sounded like someone had left a radio on, garbled and overly loud. "Think of how proud everyone will be. . . . I know you can do it. . . . Besides . . . you have to do it. . . . You won't be able to spend time with your husband . . . when he comes for family week. . . . You know what you need to do. . . . Your girls are counting on you. . . . They will be so proud of their mommy. . . ."

The buzzing of her words faded as I took my hands away from my face and turned to look at her. My eyes were no longer filled with tears. They were flashing with malevolence. She appeared slightly alarmed.

"Excuse me," I said slowly. "Did you just mention my husband and my children?" She began to inch farther away from me. "Did I hear you say that if I eat all this food, *then* my husband and my children will be proud of me?"

She floundered around for an adequate response. "Well, strictly speaking," she explained, "I said that if you ate all the food, you would be able to spend time with your husband and that your children would be proud of the effort you are making to get better."

I narrowed my eyes at her.

"I'm sure that they are very proud of you," she added quickly. "I mean, you're here, in treatment, after all . . ."

Intense hatred and loathing were blazing from me, hotter than the flames of King Nebuchadnezzar's fiery furnace.

"Okay," I said. "I'll eat it."

She watched me incredulously as I shoveled the food in my mouth. I could tell she was trying to smooth things over. "Great job," she said. "I knew you could do it."

"Yes," I said. "You knew I could do it." She surveyed me as if my mind had come unhinged.

The meal ended and I cleared my tray. I took my handcrafted place mat and unceremoniously shoved it in the trash can. I then walked straight over to the phone. I didn't know if I had permission at that point in time to use the phone, but that was irrelevant to me. I called my husband, who I knew had taken the kids to my grandmother's house for Thanksgiving. He answered the phone, and I explained how hard the day had been for me.

"Could I please come home?" I asked.

I knew deep down that I couldn't really come home. I had too much pride and too much to lose by leaving. I knew I needed to stay the course. But right then I desperately wanted to hear him say that he felt sorry for me, that he knew I was a prisoner in an unjust war, that I had been wronged by being incarcerated, and that he would support whatever I would decide to do. I wanted him to acknowledge that, as I was speaking to him, in that very moment, I could hear the sounds of my children in the background, I could see the familiar rooms of my grandmother's house, I could feel the warmth of the sun as it shone through the big bay window in the front room, filling the room with nostalgic comfort; I could feel the vast separation between me and my family, between reality and my own sham-reality. That was what I needed from him in that moment.

But no. My pitiful, unbridled need for comfort collided with tough love. He said that he was there and I was here, that this was a day to celebrate gratitude, and that I should be grateful for the opportunity to get better.

I hung up the phone and walked straight past the long rows of now-empty tables, the orange-and-yellow tablecloths bunched and stained, hanging sadly off the sides, and walked out the back door. Walking out of any door, whether it was back, front, or side, just after a meal, without permission and unsupervised was strictly forbidden. That was the unbreakable rule of all rules. But rules and regulations meant nothing to me at that moment. I didn't consider what I was doing or where I was going; I just knew I wanted out. Out of everything. Out of a marriage that didn't seem to matter anymore, out of this treatment center in the middle of this godforsaken desert. And Godforsaken was how I truly felt. I walked onto a dirt road, and I started crying again. The dust in the air turned the tears streaming down my face into muddy streaks.

I walked and I walked and I walked until I came to the front gates. Walking out the side door was forbidden, so walking out through the front gates was an unpardonable crime. At any moment someone would be coming to try to collect me. Sure enough, a van drove up behind me, filled with treatment workers trying to reason with me to come back. They explained that while they were not allowed to physically force me to return, if I didn't *choose* to come back, all sorts of pain, calamity, and misfortune would fall upon me.

Ha! I laughed in their faces. It was a mocking, derisive laugh. I knew there was nothing they could do to force me to go back. There was not a person on the face of the earth who could force me to do what I did not want to do. I simply kept walking. Every once in a while, one of the workers would get out of the van and try to catch up with me. But they could not catch me. "They don't know who they are dealing with," I thought. I was power walking as though my life depended on it. The faster I walked away from that horrible place, the faster I would be able to regain autonomy over my life, autonomy that had been so cruelly taken from me. I power walked into town, to the only place in town open that Thanksgiving Day, a McDonald's. I asked a person standing in line if I could pretty please borrow their cell phone.

I dialed John's number. I felt immensely satisfied. Not only had I gotten a good workout in with all of that walking, I had shown him and everyone else who was really in charge. He answered the phone. I could hear my beautiful children in the background. I could hear my mother's and my grandmother's voices. I could picture every detail. It was the Thanksgiving I should be having. John said he needed to step outside so he could hear me better. I told him I had run away and I wasn't going back.

He went crazy. He sounded like a wounded animal. Gut-wrenching pain was etched in every syllable of every word he said. He was experiencing pain that was almost indecent to witness.

I couldn't bear to hear anymore. What had I done? Why had I done it? How could I have willfully done this? What had possessed me to act so destructively? I was in so much pain, but so was he. He was the one who had been left at home alone to bear the full responsibility of raising our children. And managing the possibility of life without me in it. I didn't feel vindicated—I felt ashamedly out of control. Walking through the desert hadn't given me what I wanted. I didn't even know what it was I wanted anymore. Being in control of my weight and escaping the embarrassment of being in treatment had promised me satisfaction. They delivered nothing but emptiness.

As I listened to John's suffering and his sorrow, I saw him standing once again in the snow covered garden-of broken-down-vehicles, reaching out his hands to cup my face, to kiss me, to tell me he loved me, to beg me, "Please, let me love you." Thirteen years of a life together welled up inside me. John hadn't been able to save me. I wanted him to, but he couldn't. Years of pain and anger and shame rose up and spilled down my cheeks. With heartrending clarity, I realized that there are some things in life we can't be saved from. We have to save ourselves. I assured him I would go back and do what I needed to do. I loved him, I truly did. I hung up the phone and returned it to the woman I had borrowed it from. She surveyed me with incredulity, sadness, and a little bit of revulsion. She turned around and ordered a number two Extra Value Meal, and I steeled my resolve to meet the posse I knew would be waiting for me.

THE FALSE KING

Absalom was riding on his mule when he happened to meet David's soldiers. When the mule went under the tangled branches of a large oak tree, Absalom's head was caught fast in the tree. The mule under him kept going, so he was suspended in midair. One of the men saw him and informed Joab, "I just saw Absalom hanging in an oak tree."

"You just saw him!" Joab exclaimed. "Why didn't you strike him to the ground right there?…"

Joab said, "I'm not going to waste time with you!" He then took three spears in his hands and thrust them into Absalom's heart while he was still alive in the oak tree, and 10 young men who were Joab's armor-bearers struck him, and killed him.

Afterwards, Joab blew the ram's horn, and the troops broke off their pursuit of Israel because Joab restrained them. They took Absalom, threw him into a large pit in the forest, and piled a huge mound of stones over him. And all Israel fled, each to his tent.

When he was alive, Absalom erected for himself a pillar in the King's Valley, for he had said, "I have no son to preserve the memory of my name." So he gave the pillar his name. It is still called Absalom's Monument to this day.

2 Samuel 18:9-11, 14-18

Absalom was one of David's sons. And Absalom had wanted to be king. He wanted to wrest the position from his father David, who had been appointed king by God Himself. Decades before, in the town of Bethlehem, the prophet Samuel took the flask of oil that he had brought with him and anointed David as the king of Israel. In that sacred moment, the Spirit of the Lord came powerfully upon David. God had just singled him out with complete surety. There was no doubt. Samuel had been sent to Bethlehem with God's direction, to the house of Jesse, David's father. Samuel was on a divine mission with one purpose: to anoint one of Jesse's sons to be the next king of Israel. And the son God had chosen was David.

There is, perhaps, no more inspiring glimpse into the working of the mind of God than how He instructed Samuel to choose the man who would be the next king. Samuel was first inclined to select the tallest, most impressive-appearing man in the room. "But the Lord said to Samuel, 'Do not look at his appearance or his stature, because I have rejected him. Man does not see what the Lord sees, for man sees what is visible, but the Lord sees the heart'" (1 Samuel 16:7). This truth about the character of God is of immeasurable comfort. It reassures us, even today, **God does not place any importance on what the world values.** That is a truth on which we can build our lives. But even more so, the selection and anointing of David demonstrated that God had placed His seal of approval, His blessing, and the unmatched power of His Holy Spirit on what He had found in the heart of David.

David famously killed the bloodthirsty giant, Goliath, whose size and stature stood in grotesque contrast to his own. His battle cry reverberated throughout the nation of Israel, "Just who is this uncircumcised Philistine that he should defy the armies of the living God?" (1 Samuel 17:26). As the giant lay miraculously slain on the field of battle, David became a warrior of great renown, whose heart and actions reflected that he was consumed with divine purpose and divine perspective.

Inspired by David's astonishing victory, the Israelite army went on to rout the Philistine army and plunder their camp. David was made "commander over the men of war, an appointment that was welcomed by the people. . . . David continued to succeed in everything that he did, for the Lord was with him. . . . All Israel and Judah loved David because he was so successful at leading his troops into battle" (1 Samuel 18:5, 14, 16, nlt). Every time the Philistines attacked, David prevailed. "So David's name became very famous" (1 Samuel 18:30, nlt). His name had unparalleled fame as a warrior. He was bold and daring and courageous. He was unafraid to accept any mission that was presented to him. David placed complete confidence in the knowledge that the Spirit of the Lord was with him and would lead him to victory.

It was with this reputation as a victor that he finally took the throne as the king of Judah and ultimately, as the king over all of Israel. David was thirty years old when he finally began his reign (2 Samuel 5:4). He was no longer a ruddy-faced boy standing alone in defense of the armies of the living God. He was a man on whom the Spirit of the Lord rested, and he had the singular honor of being described as a man after God's own heart.

David was also the father of many children. Despite his heavenly job appointment, his household was quite a dysfunctional mess. His third born son, the aforementioned Absalom, murdered his brother Amnon, the firstborn and heir to the throne. He killed him in an act of self-justified vengeance because Amnon had raped his half sister, Tamar. Amnon had indeed committed the repugnant act, worthy of punishment. Incredibly, David was unable to bring himself to discipline Amnon for this reprehensible crime. Absalom determined he would not be weak like his father and proceeded to carry out justice on his own terms. With the decision to murder his brother, he set a precedent by which he would live his life: he was above all, he answered to no one, and he wanted to be king.

Absalom began to formulate a plan to slowly subvert and discredit David in order to attempt to seize to the throne. After he murdered his brother, he immediately fled the country. For three years, he waited for the chance to return to Israel. He waited until David had come to terms with Amnon's death and was longing to see Absalom again. Upon hearing this report, Absalom returned to Jerusalem, living in the same city as his father, expecting at any moment to hear from his father. David never summoned him. The fact that his father, the king, had not summoned him or wanted to see him, seemed to have deeply wounded Absalom's escalating sense of entitlement.

Absalom stood out, far above other people. In fact, he was regarded and praised as the most handsome man in all of Israel. "No man in all Israel was as handsome and highly praised as Absalom. From the sole of his foot to the top of his head, he did not have a single flaw. When he shaved his head—he shaved it every year because his hair got so heavy for him that he had to shave it off—he would weigh the hair from his head, and it would be five pounds according to the royal standard" (2 Samuel 14:25-26). He was magnificent, and everyone knew it . . . except, apparently, the king. The flame of rebellion might have risen out of the unanswered-for crime against his sister, but it was the years it took for David to see his murderous son that brought the consuming fire of war into the house of David.

Absalom had bided his time, years of it, and now he was poised to make his true intentions known. He would get up early every morning and station his magnificent self at the gates of the city. His plan was to steal the hearts of the people. He was good-looking, and he went around on a chariot with fifty bodyguards. He painted himself as the picture of mercy and understanding. When people came to the gate of the city, they would tell Absalom they were there to present a case to the king for judgment. Absalom would respond, in complete dishonesty, that the king didn't have anyone who would be able to do that for them.

"If only someone would appoint me judge in the land," he pontificated. "Then anyone who had a grievance or dispute could come to me, and I would make sure he received justice" (2 Samuel 15:4). He would never allow people to bow before him. "When a person approached to bow down to him, Absalom reached out his hand, took hold of him, and kissed him" (2 Samuel 15:5). His charisma and trickery produced the desired result. The people loved him and began to withdraw their allegiance to his father and give their hearts to him.

The conspiracy gained momentum. Absalom brazenly spread the false message that he had been crowned king in Hebron. He set himself up as king and proceeded to commit unspeakable acts to demonstrate and underscore that he did not desire reconciliation with his father, the true king. He desired David's destruction. Absalom was a grasping, devious usurper who used violence, defiance, and shameless perversion to attempt to achieve his goal: He wanted to kill the true king and rule in his place.

It didn't end well for Absalom. A battle raged in the forest of Ephraim between the armies of David and the armies loyal to Absalom, and it was there that Absalom became entangled in the branch of the oak. Hanging helplessly in a tree, imprisoned by his own beautiful, magnificent hair, he met his violent demise.

History is full of accounts of usurpers—sometimes they succeed, sometimes they fail. Absalom was not unique in his ambition or his action. He was also not unique in the fundamental belief by which he lived his life, a belief shared by every usurper, past or present. It is the idea that they can obtain something that is not rightfully theirs. Every usurper clings so deeply to this idea, that they are being denied something that is rightfully theirs, that they are willing to attempt to possess what they are being denied . . . by any means necessary.

Usurpers take what is not theirs.

Usurpers will go to any lengths to establish a kingdom built by and for themselves.

Usurpers are consumed with power and terrified of weakness.

Usurpers do not compromise. They stubbornly advance their objectives.

Usurpers pursue their own glory, whatever the cost to anyone else.

Usurpers prey upon the brokenhearted, those who believe that they are not enough.

Usurpers promise justice, vengeance, love, and fulfillment, but instead, leave you alone in a treatment center, separated from your children, bereft of any hope.

Usurpers cause you to run away into the desert because you are convinced that freedom from an eating disorder is a lost cause. And that change is simply not possible . . .

This brings me back to that day in the desert. I had run as fast as I could from the treatment center to attempt to escape the crushing absoluteness of life with an eating disorder, only to collide with the usurper. The moment I listened to my husband's sorrow and comprehended the depth of his unbearable pain, I came face-to-face with the reality of the usurper: **My flesh.**

MY FLESH IS THE USURPER!

The usurper is my flesh, the part of me that strives to find its fulfillment apart from the mercy and grace and love of God. I had let the usurper obtain what was rightfully mine. And what was rightfully mine was a life led by the Spirit, not a life enslaved to the flesh. With that realization, I experienced a moment of clarity and saw that I was not in control. At all.

As I penitently allowed myself to be collected by the swarm of treatment workers, I began to understand that I had been living according to a false king's edicts. And my flesh was indeed a false king. Just as the people of Israel had listened to Absalom, I had listened to my flesh's soothing flattery: "If I were king, you wouldn't have to bow to me! I'll share my power with you. You no longer have to be at the mercy of others!" I had been dazzled by the usurper's beauty. I had believed the flesh's deceit: "You've got a strong case here! It's too bad the real king won't hear it. If I were judge, I'd understand how hard life really has been for you, and how very hard you've been trying to overcome the unjust pain of your past." I had let myself get caught up in a rumor. "Have you not heard that there is another king—a BETTER king!" I had believed that the usurper, my flesh, maybe, just maybe, really was the true king.

The usurper promised me happiness, confidence, acceptance, health, freedom from fear, relief from pain, contentment, peace, joy, and purpose. But those were empty promises. The usurper, my flesh, could never deliver on them. He does not have the authority. He claims to be king, but he is not. He is a twisted imitation, a distorted copy of a real king. He is a tyrant, a dictator of the vilest kind. His false government exists for but one purpose—death and destruction of all but himself.

The flesh desires what is contrary to the Spirit. It provides a way to cope with life when life is just too hard to bear. But the coping mechanism it provides is rebellious and hostile to God. God's Kingdom is built on a foundation of limitless truth and unconditional love, but the usurper builds his kingdom on a foundation of cleverly devised lies and relentless shame. The flesh whispers in the shadows of despair, "If you just don't eat, you will be thin. And when you are thin, you will be happy. When you are thin, you will be attractive. When you are thin, someone will love you. When you are thin, you will have confidence to face the future."

The flesh presents its case to be the new king in moments when the real king seems far-off, when the true king seems like a father who doesn't know how to love or like a mythical hero of old who is too good to really be true. The usurper, the flesh, comes in moments of pain and insecurity and doubt and abuse and failure and rejection and shame, vowing to save you and take away your suffering once and for all.

Let me tell you this: There is only one True King. He is King over every usurper. He won't turn away in the face of injustice. He will never leave you to face your hurt alone.

He made you.

And He loves you.

CHAPTER 7

Have You Ever Felt the Earth Breathe?

Backward, turn backward, O Time, in thy flight,
Make me a child again, just for to-night!

ELIZABETH AKERS ALLEN

One summer evening, when I was an eight-year-old girl, I lay down, stretching myself out on the grass in my backyard, and felt the breath of the earth. The grass was fragrant with the sweet coolness of the fast-descending night. Fireflies were appearing, rising from the ground like sparks from a fire, then fading away like dying embers. I lay gazing at the sky, binoculars in one hand, half-eaten chocolate bar in the other. I broke off a piece and ate it, putting the binoculars to my eyes to gain a clearer view of the sky. The stars intensified in visibility. I shoved the rest of the chocolate bar in my mouth and continued to gaze heavenward. As I gazed at the darkening sky, beholding the multitude of the starry host, I began to do one of my favorite things: Imagining.

I imagined that I was the earth. I was lost, separated from my long-ago friends, the stars. I imagined I could see them, but they could not see me, for they still had the power of fire, but I had lost mine when I fell and found myself wandering in this dark galaxy. I imagined that although I had lost my firepower, I still had the power of my voice, and that was the only means of communication that was left for me to try to contact them.

As I lay pressed against the damp night grass, I took a deep breath, and the earth breathed, because I was the earth. I sang, and the earth sang, because I was the earth. I was a lonely melody rising from darkened canyons, from misty-faced mountains, from oceans deep and roiling, from forest floors shrouded in shade. I sang louder, in a mournful wail, "Friends where are you? Why do you hide?"

Suddenly, the stars seemed to grow a bit brighter. Encouraged by this development, I continued singing. The louder I sang, the more brilliant the stars appeared. I sang louder still, and the tiny points of light burst into flame, into beacons of fire. They had heard me! They had heard me! I sat up and dropped the binoculars aside. I squeezed my eyes closed tight and felt the earth beneath my chocolate-covered fingers.

The next morning, I jumped out of bed and ran to the kitchen door to look out at the backyard, which the night before had been the scene of so much magic and wonder. The earth looked unassuming, quiet and still, fresh-scrubbed in the morning sun. My mom was pouring milk in my bowl of cereal, a glass of orange juice already placed beside it on the table. I turned from the door and sat down at the breakfast table to eat. It was morning and I was hungry. I had a full day of adventure and exploration ahead of me, after all. I needed energy to do such things. I finished eating, put my dishes in the sink, yelled, "I love you!" and was out the door.

The beginning of the day is a magnificent time when you are a child and the entirety of your responsibility is to live life to the fullest. Innocence and imagination are beautiful, sacred things. But when you are a child, you don't ponder the existence of such things because you are too busy living them. As I ran out of the kitchen door on that summer morning, I wasn't thinking about savoring innocence and imagination. I was immersed in the task before me: rooting through the garden tools in the garage, searching for the shovel. I uncovered what I was looking for and grabbed it. Rusty spade in hand, I marched over to the edge of the empty lot that bordered my own backyard. I surveyed the lot and saw an expanse of uncharted territory, ripe for exploration. As I looked out over the lot, covered in a tangle of grass and clover, dandelion and lady slippers, innocent imagination seized me.

Shouldering the shovel, I imagined that I was going to dig myself an underground palace. I stood imagining the subterranean majesty of my underground palace until the sky turned from clean, sparkling blue to washed out and pale from the heat of the summer sun. I wiped the perspiration from my forehead and began to imagine something else: I imagined if I ran home right now, I could somehow convince my mom to make some grape Kool-Aid!

As a little girl, I moved from one adventure to another. My body was a vehicle to those adventures, and food was fuel for the vehicle. I didn't think about my body any farther than what I could be doing with it: digging, jumping, cartwheeling, swimming, singing, spinning, dancing, climbing, and on and on. I didn't think about food beyond its delicious and necessary role in fueling my daily enterprises. When I was hungry, I ate. When I wasn't, I didn't. Unless I was given money to spend at the penny candy store. Or if I heard the ice cream truck. Or if I could make a sandwich with three kinds of cheese!

At those moments, food was nourishment for a body that was growing and active, but it was also family, fun, love, comfort, and enjoyment. Food was all of those things and more—an ingredient of experiencing living life to the fullest. This is how food should be seen. Food is a good creation, **provided by a good God, for me.** The fact that this is true bears much repeating.

God designed and created food for us, to be partaken and enjoyed, together with all of creation. And it was very good.

Now the serpent was the most cunning of all the wild animals that the Lord God had made. He said to the woman, "Did God really say, 'You can't eat from any tree in the garden?'"

The woman said to the serpent, "We may eat the fruit from the trees in the garden. But about the fruit of the tree in the middle of the garden, God said,'You must not eat it or touch it, or you will die.'"

"No! You will not die," the serpent said to the woman. "In fact, God knows that when you eat it your eyes will be opened, and you will be like God, knowing good and evil."

Then the woman saw that the tree was good for food and delightful to look at, and that it was desirable for obtaining wisdom. So she took some of its fruit and ate it; she also gave some to her husband, who was with her, and he ate it. Then the eyes of both of them were opened, and they knew they were naked; so they sewed fig leaves together and made loincloths for themselves.
Genesis 3:1-7

With the words of the serpent's beguiling ringing in their ears, Adam and Eve believed a lie: God was unreasonable and jealous— He did not truly want what was best for them. They believed that they could somehow control and overcome circumstances they did not understand. They believed the lie that they could eat of the tree of the knowledge of good and evil and, by so doing, obtain something rightfully theirs, but being withheld by an unjust God. They believed lies and acted according to them. And creation fell.

Just as Adam and Eve could not stay unashamed in the Garden of Eden after the Fall, walking and talking with the living God, so my healthy view of food and my belief that my body was a vehicle, could not stay, either.

Nature's first green is gold,
Her hardest hue to hold.
Her early leaf's a flower;
But only so an hour.
Then leaf subsides to leaf.
So Eden sank to grief,
So dawn goes down to day.
Nothing gold can stay.
Robert Frost

At the age of seventeen I sank into grief. As I sat with an un-opened lunch in my lap, lies began to seduce me. Lies that said by controlling what I ate, I could somehow manage what was utterly unmanageable. That God had failed me . . . and that I had failed Him . . . so badly. That my body was no longer fit to be a vehicle for adventures, but rather, it was a traitor. It was shameful. And I ought to be ashamed of it. Lovely promises beguiled me—hunger was a cure for guilt and being thin was the key to being fulfilled. After all, if losing a little weight brought happiness, then losing a lot of weight was unimaginable joy.

Golden days of wonder and imagination were gone, usurped by a new, false reality. Food no longer was nourishment, family, com-fort, and pleasure; it was a disgusting necessity, wrought with fear and shame. My body no longer was a vehicle, but a master, cruel and demanding. The little girl with a shovel and a fearless imagina-tion had vanished into memory. Faded away, as dawn goes down to day.

Lies are bewitching things. Especially ones that have a good deal of truth mixed in. At the age of seventeen, I considered the depth of my own shortcomings, the entirety of my insufficiencies, and I began to make choices based on lies. With each new choice to starve or binge or purge or pretend or manipulate, the usurper grew ever stronger. I pledged my allegiance to a false king. As the usurper grew in power and influence, I diminished. I lost any sense of what I used to be, of what food used to be to me. What food should have been. I had thrown happiness and true contentment away, reaching out for the whisper of a fraudulent promise. Exchanging the truth of what food and my body were for a lie.

A magnificent, hideous lie.

A PLACE TO STAND

I sat on a bench overlooking a dry and dusty vista, which incidentally was just outside the infamous back door through which I had made my Thanksgiving jailbreak. Yes, I was still there, the day after my attempted exodus into the desert. The little girl who had once stood before an empty lot on a golden summer day was gone. In her place, was a dejected mother standing on the edge of a vastly different, empty landscape. Parched hills covered in loose rock and scraggly brush rose up from the brown earth. They were bleak and barren. I could not see any beauty or possibility there, hidden beneath the tumbleweed-covered expanse, dotted with cactus and mesquite. They were drab and lifeless. The years spent believing lies had long since choked the imagination that said treasure and wonder could be concealed below an ordinary surface.

Hope was on the horizon, however. My husband would arrive the next week to participate in family week with me. Since the Thanksgiving debacle, I had decided to toe the line in treatment. Nothing would come between my ability to see him when he came. With my therapist, I had been working on my personal inventory, examining past patterns of behavior and past hurts to determine if there were any common threads or themes from which I could glean knowledge. I would share that knowledge with my husband during family week, and he would do likewise with me.

The day finally arrived. I couldn't believe he was there, present in the midst of the desert of my misery. Seeing him made me feel almost human again; he held me in his arms and we sat together on the bench overlooking the rocky terrain. We both sat there, drinking in the possibility that change was imminent. The week to come would galvanize us and unite us together. Or so we hoped. This was, after all, our last hope. We had tried everything we had known to try. We had exhausted all other resources.

Things needed to change now, or they never would.

We understood this full well when we climbed out of the van that had transported us from the treatment center to the family counseling center, where we would engage in family week. Our therapist was someone I had never seen before, and he was very good at his job; adept at helping us navigate the treacherous waters of blame and responsibility, of what went wrong and how it could be fixed.

We were making some headway, but it was slow going. The whole week was tediously moving us along toward an event that was slated to happen at the very end: an event called "Truth in Love." This was a moment for which we both were anxiously waiting, the moment we could share, uninterrupted, our own personal hurts and struggles regarding the other person. We each had written down some specific ways that the other had hurt us. We were supposed to describe what they had done, in detail, and how it had made us feel. All of this would happen under the guidance of the therapist.

Finally the moment arrived. I was trembling with emotion, and I could see that my husband was doing the same. We sat in chairs facing one another. I unfolded my paper and began to read first.

"I feel hurt when I try to tell you how I feel and you respond by trying to counsel me and fix me." The exercise continued: I would tell him how I felt and he would try to understand and see what he could do to change. "I feel hopeless when you become cold and distant when I admit that I have messed up."

I could see he was really trying to respond without becoming too defensive. Finally I said, "I feel humiliated when you talk to me as if I am one of your therapy clients."

This exchange where I listed my grievances and he responded seemed to go fairly well, but I kept noticing that from time to time he would look down at his paper, which was crammed full with minuscule writing. After he would look at it, he would look up at me with feverish excitement in his eyes. I could see what he was waiting for—*his* turn.

At last, his moment arrived. He smoothed his paper and prepared to read the indictment. Then, just as he had barely begun to present his case, he was interrupted.

"Oh, I am so sorry. I had no idea what time it was. I'm afraid we will not have time for you to read your Truth in Love, John," our therapist cut across him.

John just sat there, mouthing wordlessly, lifting his paper and gesturing to it over and over again. He blurted out, "But I've been waiting and waiting for this moment. This isn't fair!" He was quivering with indignation at the injustice of the situation. It wasn't fair. It was unbelievably unfair and I, beholding the sheer outrage on his face, agreed. But I could do nothing about it. I was powerless to change what had just happened. John's expression became inscrutable. I had a feeling of dread in the pit of my stomach. I was afraid this turn of events had just cost me my marriage.

We took a break, during which I was required to eat a snack. John and I sat down together at a table and I spread my portion of trail mix out on a napkin in front of me. He sat there in stony silence. I knew what his indifference meant—he had reached the limit of what he was able to handle. He was done trying. It was over. I finished my snack and crumpled the napkin up. Despondency spread through my entire being.

This was the end. All the struggle and the hurt and the striving and the wide-eyed reckless hope had been for nothing. We had reached the point of no return. As I sat beside my husband, in the very last session of family week, I, as Nathaniel Hawthorne wrote, "could no longer borrow from the future to help [myself] through [my] present grief." That moment, sitting in a folding chair, feeling the cold metal against my skin, was perhaps the most hopeless I have ever felt in my life. Not only was I trapped from that day forward and forevermore in slavery to the eating disorder, but I had lost everything else as well. I alone was to blame. I felt as if I couldn't breathe.

But then, that wonderful, wonderful man who was our therapist stood up and informed us that he was going to do one final exercise with us. It was, in fact, something he loathed to do. He practically asked for our forgiveness prior to starting.

He started speaking, only his voice did not sound normal. It was low and harsh; it sounded positively evil. I thought it was a joke. A sick and twisted joke. He spoke to us as though the eating disorder were talking to us. He recounted his delight in all he had taken from us. At this point I no longer believed it was a joke; I was riveted in horror. He listed all the ways he was going to continue to ruin our lives and our futures. He taunted us, reveling in how he had gotten me to believe every word he had ever said, how I had been his victim and his prisoner for all of those years. Finally, with words straight from the pit of hell, he described how he was going to get our little daughters next.

We just sat there. My eyes were burning with tears. I felt revulsion in the pit of my stomach like the pains of childbirth. My husband was looking straight ahead, past the therapist, past anything that was happening presently. He kept looking and looking and looking; at what I didn't know. After what seemed like hours, he turned and looked at me, and I could have never, *never,* prepared myself for what he was about to say.

"It's not you," John said, his voice breaking. "You are not the eating disorder. I have been so angry at you, and all this time I should have been angry at the eating disorder."

It was as if, for just a moment, a veil was pulled away and we both saw a little girl. And it was not her fault. She was not the enemy. She was worth fighting for. As John spoke those words to me, I felt something that I had not felt for a very long time. I felt Imagination.

I closed my eyes, and the walls of the center dissolved to blue sky. I was a little girl standing on the edge of an empty field, my heart captivated with daring certainty that the earth was deeper than it was wide and that there was an underground palace in there, waiting to be uncovered. I could hear the earth breathe, *Anything is possible.* Anything . . . health, forgiveness, restoration, love, hope, peace, change, transformation, they were all possible. Something cataclysmic had just shifted. The foundation on which I had constructed my entire lonely existence crumbled in an instant. It wasn't only up to me to change; we were in this together.

And anything was possible.

Two things changed that day. I can say with absolute certainty that these two things directly contributed to my victory over my eating disorder. The first thing was that, for the first time, I felt like we were in the fight together. John no longer believed it was only up to me. He had said so many times before, "If only you would change, then things would be different." Or, "Don't you want to be happy? Then just stop!"

The second thing was that we identified a common enemy. And that enemy's name was not Jennene. It was Eating Disorder . It was the part of me that had been seeking to find fulfillment in something other than in the grace and mercy of God. It was the usurper, my flesh. It was the dictator that had been on a bloody quest to totally dominate my soul and then kill my body. It was all the desires that warred against my spirit, influencing every misguided decision I made about food. It was the traitorous tyrant to whom I had been giving my allegiance.

Yes, treachery in the Garden of Eden ran deep and creation fell. Yes, I had made a litany of bad choices, too numerous to count, which had led me to the brink of ruin. Yes, the power of the usurper had overshadowed the healthy view of food and the belief that my body was a vehicle. Yes, it was true: "Dawn goes down to day. / Nothing gold can stay." All of that was true.

But this verse from Edmund Spenser was also true: "For whatsoever from one place doth fall, / Is with the tide unto another brought: / For there is nothing lost, that may be found if sought." Jesus came to seek and save that which was lost. From the time of Eden until that very day in the treatment center, when I recognized the Truth; Jesus had been relentlessly pursuing that which had been lost . . . Jesus had been pursuing me. He pursued me to that moment in family week when I began to believe this Truth: I was not the eating disorder, and there is nothing lost that cannot be found. There is nothing lost that cannot be redeemed. The cross of Christ proved that. Though the enormity of the lie I believed was great, the Truth was even greater.

And the Truth was worth fighting for.

Armed with this knowledge, in a family therapy center in the middle of the desert, I planted my feet to stand; as David once stood before the armies of the Philistines, stepping out to face the giant Goliath. "You come against me with a dagger, spear, and sword, but I come against you in the name of the Lord of Hosts, the God of the Israel's armies—you have defied Him" (1 Samuel 17:45).

The eating disorder was a usurper. It had been exposed and identified as a false king. Knowing that and believing that gave me a place to stand.

I was preparing to wage holy war on an unholy adversary.

CHAPTER 8

Spiritual Warfare

Satan promises the best, but pays with the worst;
he promises honour, and pays with disgrace; he promises pleasure,
and pays with pain; he promises profit, and pays with loss;
he promises life, and pays with death. But God pays as he promises;
all his payments are made in pure gold.

CHARLES SPURGEON

You may have only heard of spiritual warfare in terms of our fight as believers versus the devil. In most presentations or teachings about spiritual warfare, the devil gets all the attention. I've even been told that I must have been possessed by a demon because of my struggle. Years ago, while in the throes of my eating disorder, I sat in a church service, hoping to find help, or at least encouragement to keep on fighting the good fight. Instead of hearing words of hope, I was forced to listen to a pompous evangelist declare, "The reason that there is no cure for anorexia and bulimia is because they are demons!" He was pumping his fists and strutting about.

As he made this pronouncement, condemnation filled my entire being. This all-encompassing judgment reinforced what I had always been told: there was something lacking in me, or in the quality of my belief, that prevented me from experiencing victory. If someone would have told me at that point in my life I was possessed by the devil, I would have most likely agreed. I was so overwhelmed with guilt and was floundering around so desperately for answers, *any* answer, I would have accepted that diagnosis with the appropriate level of shame and resignation.

To follow that line of thinking, it would have been reasonable to conclude that if the devil were responsible, then I needed to defeat the devil to make the eating disorder (aka the demon) go away. I needed to war against the devil and all the forces of hell, name it and claim it. I needed to defeat and overcome the devil, be healed, and move on with my life. But the problem with that line of reasoning was that, well . . . the devil already was defeated.

Now since the children have flesh and blood in common, He also shared in these, so that through His death He might destroy the one holding the power of death—the Devil—and free those who were held in slavery all their lives by the fear of death. Hebrews 2:14-15

God secured victory over the devil when He sent His one and only Son to suffer and die in our place and be raised to life, defeating death, hell, and the grave. "Resist the Devil, and he will flee" (James 4:7). I truly do not wish or intend to minimize or degrade the despicable enemy that the devil is. He is dangerous and he is dedicated to our destruction. "He was a murderer from the beginning and has not stood in the truth, because there is no truth in him. When he tells a lie he speaks from his own nature, because he is a liar and the father of lies" (John 8:44). There is not a lie that does not originate with him. I know that very well.

I also know that I used to give him way too much credit in the past when attempting to fight against my eating disorder. I gave the devil too much credit because I believed that if I raised my spiritual defenses against him, then my eating disorder would stop. Hadn't I always been told that the only cure for my eating disorder was a knock-down, drag-out fight with the devil and all the demons of hell?

The devil is a predator, a liar, and an accuser, but his rightful position has already been assigned. Jesus saw to that on the cross.

The devil is a threat—but only in cahoots with the flesh. Only when my flesh participates in his plans. Because I am a believer in Jesus Christ, the devil has no authority over me. He only has influence if I give it to him by listening to his lies and beginning to act as if I believed them. "Walk by the Spirit, and you *will not* carry out the desire of the flesh" (Galatians 5:16, emphasis added). If you walk by the Spirit, the flesh will be subdued and the devil has no foothold. *If the flesh is subdued, the devil has no foothold!*

At this juncture, it is worth pointing out that warfare against the devil and all his principalities *does* indeed exist. When someone teaches on the devil and spiritual warfare, this conundrum usually exists: people tend to ascribe old Beelzebub too much power, or too little power—some go so far as denying his very existence. Satan *does* exist and his forces *do* in fact war against the forces of God. There is a fight happening, unseen by human eyes, between the forces of the living God and the forces of darkness. But insofar as this warfare affects our lives as believers—the devil versus us—Satan's power is notoriously overstated. He is the prince of this world. Not the prince of the believers. The devil and all the fury of hell may rage in this world, but we, as believers in the Son of the living God, are not subject to his tyranny.

British evangelist Smith Wigglesworth (1859–1947) is attributed with telling this story about an interaction he and his wife, Polly, had with the devil.

We were sleeping one night, when the manifestation of evil filled the room and the spirit of fear gripped both of us. Polly was so frightened she could not open her eyes. I suddenly sat up, in the bed, and saw the devil. I rubbed my eyes to be sure, it was him. I said, "Oh, it's only you." I then turned to Polly and told her to go back to sleep, it was nothing of consequence, and I laid my head back down. Suddenly an overwhelming sense of peace and love filled the room and we had the most blessed sleep ever.

Smith Wigglesworth recognized the devil was no match for the power that lived inside him as a believer—the same power that raised Christ from the dead. The devil was already defeated and should be treated as such. That was the extent of Smith Wigglesworth's spiritual warfare against the devil's personal threat to him as a believer in Christ.

This brings me back to my original position. There is in fact a whole other front in this spiritual war that gets very little playtime in the spiritual warfare anthology. It is the war between us and the evil desires that tempt us. Or as I have referred to it, the war against the usurper, the flesh.

From this point on, when I refer to warfare, I will be referring to warring against the flesh. From my experience, and according to the Word of God, engaging the flesh in spiritual warfare is entirely appropriate.

For though we live in the world, we do not wage war as the world does. The weapons we fight with are not the weapons of the world. On the contrary, they have divine power to demolish strongholds. We demolish arguments and every pretension that sets itself up against the knowledge of God, and we take captive every thought to make it obedient to Christ.
2 Corinthians 10:3-5, niv

In his book *Dressed to Kill: A Biblical Approach to Spiritual Warfare and Armor,* Rick Renner, scholar of ancient Greek, wrote,

"Of the five times that the words 'war' and 'warfare,' taken from the word *stratos,* are used in the New Testament, they are *never once* used in connection with the devil."

James 4:1 uses the word *war* to describe "the cravings that are at war within you". In other words, the flesh.

Throughout my life, spiritual warfare brought to mind my insufficiencies, my lack of faith, my decades-long losing streak to the devil. But as I became aware of the usurper's malicious presence in my life, it was increasingly harder to accept the false reality that I, as a believer in Jesus, struggled with an eating disorder because I was losing to the devil or possessed by a demon. Jesus already won the victory over an enemy I could have never defeated no matter how hard I tried, so the question no longer was "How do I defeat the devil?" but "How do I fight the flesh?" The blood shed on the cross rendered the enemy powerless. Yet he had one trick still up his sleeve. He could ally with my flesh, the usurper, through deceit and destroy the work of God in me.

How could I fight *me?*

CHAPTER 9

Preparing to Fight

Love is not love
Which alters when it alteration finds,
Or bends with the remover to remove:
O, no! it is an ever-fixed mark,
That looks on tempests, and is never shaken . . .

SONNET 116, WILLIAM SHAKESPEARE

To be successful in achieving something, you have to *want it*. If your goal is better health, you have to *want it*. If your heart's desire is to be free from food issues, you have to *want it*. Treatment will never deliver its promised results unless you *want it enough*. You have to *want to stop* acting the way you are acting!

How many times have I been told this? How many times have I told myself this? How many times have *you* been told this? How many times have you told this to yourself? *You have to want it.* There is much truth in this statement. If I don't want to change, there isn't a power on the face of the earth that can make me. I discovered this immutable truth with disturbing clarity when I was in inpatient treatment.

I kept discovering it when I returned home from treatment. I wish I could say that my time in treatment "fixed" me and that when I came home, things took a turn for the better. I suppose in some ways they did; I had actually followed through with completing treatment, which was no insignificant feat. Doing this proved, to myself and to my family, that when it came down to choosing between the eating disorder and my family, I chose my family. But in some ways things took a turn for the worse. I was back at home, which was what my end goal had been, but now, everyone—and I mean everyone—knew what I struggled with. I was thrust into never before experienced levels of scrutiny and shame. This spotlight led me to act out in new and even more erratic ways.

The adversarial state of mind I displayed while in treatment was *nothing* to the rage and anger I blatantly projected on anyone and everyone in my path at home. Anger bubbled beneath the surface of every interaction I had with another human being. My children were the exception—I was in a state of depressed guilt when I was with them. Every time I looked at them, I sensed that they knew who I really was. I imagined they recognized, deep down, they deserved to have someone much better for a mother.

When I arrived home from the treatment center, I had an action and accountability plan in my hand, to be put in place (by me) immediately. This plan included continuing therapy. I grudgingly went a grand total of two times. In these sessions, the therapist looked at me with a tilted head, expression part curiosity, part grave concern, part fear.

"There's a lot of anger there . . ." His voice trailed off as he stumbled around to figure out why I was so enraged. I didn't afford him the opportunity to ask me why. This was a colossal waste of my precious time. I had made it through treatment, hadn't I? Why on earth was I required to jump through yet another set of hoops?

Looking back, I see that my anger made sense. Anger is a core emotion, after all. It is not a sin. The ways we respond and react to our anger may be sinful, but the anger itself is not. It is a gut reaction to feeling out of control. And I was devastatingly out of control at that moment in time. The raw nerve of my being had been laid bare; I was a self-maligned sideshow, adrift in a sea of scrutiny, alone and assigning blame and wrath on everything in my warpath.

I settled my fury upon a lengthy list of things. I was angry with God because He still hadn't fixed me! I had asked Him so many times to take this away and heal me, and He had not done it yet. I was angry with myself because I had allowed my eating disorder to be taken from me. I had gained weight and was out of control. I was angry with people who treated me like the contemptible spectacle I had become, whose honor-bound duty seemed to be providing a running commentary on my weight and appearance. I was angry with church people who continued to judge me and tell me if I had enough faith, I wouldn't be still struggling like this; who continued to tell me God's favor was surely not upon me because I wasn't prosperous. Oh, how I hated those church people. They sickened me to the core of my being with their slogans and trite sayings: "Everything happens for a reason." "Your body is a temple."

I fought the urge to strangle someone every time they would patronizingly say, "All things work together for good." *Do they? Do they really? That abuse I experienced isn't working out so well! The shame I have endured isn't working out so well! Looking at people and seeing judgment in their eyes isn't working out so well! The haunting memory of all the things I sacrificed on the altar of the eating disorder isn't working out so well!*

My heart was a boiling cauldron of rage. I dared not allow myself the luxury of bumping into it for fear it would overflow. This was a tricky undertaking because I was bitterly angry at so many things— but I was angriest, above all, at the eating disorder. Why would it not just leave me alone?

I wanted it to stop so badly that on the Mother's Day following my return home from treatment, I did something very public and very pitiful. It was an attempt to reach out to God and beg Him, "Please help me. I want my eating disorder to stop!"

I walked into church that morning, "World's Best Mom" pin attached to my Sunday best. One of my children had made the pin and given it to me earlier that morning as a gift. Because it was Mother's Day, the church was packed with a host of wayward children and reluctant fathers, all of whom had been compelled to go to church, just this one Sunday, by their mother or wife. Perhaps it was for that reason the pastor broke step with the usual order of the service and interrupted the singing to offer an altar call. He waited for a pause in between songs and seized that moment to issue an invitation to all who wished to find God and meet with Him.

"Please, come to the altar. God is waiting for you there!" It was a powerful moment, pregnant with possibility that the wayward children and reluctant fathers would respond to the Spirit's calling, come to the altar, and discover the love of the God of the universe there.

Several people did indeed respond and went forward; I couldn't tell you who, but I do know I was one of them. I practically ran up there, holding my baggy skirt up on my thin frame—I had immediately lost all the weight I had been forced to gain while in treatment.

Falling on the floor before the altar of God, I sobbed, "Help me! I want to change. I want this to stop. I don't want to do this anymore!" I was clutching my "World's Best Mom" pin in my hand, my lifeline to the truth. I really did want to change. I wanted to be a mother worthy of my children's emulation. I hated the eating disorder, and I believed that God was perfectly able to take it from me. Please, God, please! I was blubbering with all my might.

A woman came up beside me and was praying with me. I was experiencing a complete breakdown; I could not stop crying out to God. Nor did I want to stop. I was determined to cry out to God until He answered me.

Time went on, and I sensed the emptiness of the spaces around me as the others left the altar. The woman who had been praying with me had long since left my side. I was still there, still sobbing. It was an awkward moment. I'm sure the pastor wrestled with how to best navigate around the fact that I was stationed front and center, vociferously carrying on.

In the end he said, "If you need to remain at the altar praying, please do. We are going to continue the service. Please don't let that distract you from seeking God." They collected the offering, and he preached an entire sermon with me crumpled in a ball at the front of the church at the altar. I cried so hard and for so long my eyes were swollen shut.

My husband had to guide me out of the building when it was all said and done. We went home to celebrate Mother's Day, and I immediately acted out in my eating disorder. Mere moments after I had called out to God, so violently, so desperately, so shamefully, and in such a foolhardy way, I succumbed to my dysfunction. I had allowed the day's chain of events to accomplish the usurper's intended purpose: God was unable or unwilling to help me because I didn't believe enough. I didn't want to change badly enough. I was on the brink of complete despair. It seemed that healing and restoration were for other, better people. They certainly were not for me.

I can't even begin to describe the discouragement I felt that day. Despite my most penitent endeavors, having tried so hard to change, there I was, still enslaved. Every bit the shameful excuse for a mother as I had been before. I wanted to change. I really, really did. I even wanted to change for the right reasons. I had identified the enemy while I was in treatment, and it wasn't me. The enemy was the usurper. It was my flesh—the desires within me that warred against God, the part of me that sought to find love and fulfillment apart from the grace and mercy of God. I had identified the enemy but was no closer to throwing him down than I had been before I had started *trying* to defeat him.

Being trapped in my eating disorder had been miserable and hopeless, but at least it was safe. I could hold it close, and it was mine to manage alone. Trying to fight the usurper was uncontrollably not safe. It was unmanageable and humiliating. I couldn't imagine, in any measure, how to fight the usurper. I couldn't imagine the strategies that would lead me to victory, much less imagine victory itself. The road ahead to obtaining it was unknowable. I felt I couldn't even see my hand in front of my face, much less see where the road to fighting the usurper would lead. On that Mother's Day the usurper loomed high above me, an unbeatable foe.

That was a very dark day for me. As both a mother and a believer in Christ, I was demoralized. Later that night, as darkness settled in, I was sobbing once again, alone and on my knees, slumped over the edge of my bed. I pressed my face into the blanket and wished with all my might that God would rescue me. With every shuddering breath, I prayed He would rescue me from the fiery furnace of despair I faced, just as He had rescued Shadrach, Meshach, and Abednego from Nebuchadnezzar's flames.

THE DESIRE TO PLEASE YOU

King Nebuchadnezzar made a gold statue ninety feet tall and nine feet wide. He set it up on the plain of Dura in the province of Babylon. King Nebuchadnezzar sent word to assemble the satraps, prefects, governors, advisers, treasurers, judges, magistrates, and all the rulers of the provinces to attend the dedication of the statue the king had set up. Then they stood before the statue King Nebuchadnezzar had set up.

A herald loudly proclaimed, "People of every nation and language, you are commanded: When you hear the sound of the horn, flute, zither, lyre, harp, drum, and every kind of music, you are to fall down and worship the gold statue…but whoever does not fall down and worship will immediately be thrown into a furnace of blazing fire."

Therefore, when all the people heard the sound of…every kind of music, people of every nation and language fell down and worshipped the gold statue that King Nebuchadnezzar had set up.

Some Chaldeans took this occasion to maliciously accuse the Jews. They said to King Nebuchadnezzar, "May the King live forever…There are some Jews you have appointed to the province of Babylon: Shadrach, Meshach, and Abednego. These men have ignored you, the king. They do not serve your gods or worship the gold statue you set up."

Then in a furious rage Nebuchadnezzar gave orders to bring in Shadrach, Meshach, and Abednego. So these men were brought before the king. When they were brought in, Nebuchadnezzar asked them, "Shadrach, Meshach, and Abednego, is it true that you don't serve my gods or worship the gold statue I have set up? Now if you're ready, when you hear the sound of…every kind of music, fall down and worship the statue I have made. But if you don't worship it, you will immediately be thrown into a furnace of blazing fire—and who is the god who can rescue you from my power?"

Shadrach, Meshach, and Abednego replied to the king, *"O Nebuchadnezzar, we don't need to give you an answer to this question. If the God we serve exists, then He can rescue us from the furnace of blazing fire, and He can rescue us from the power of you, the king. But even if He does not rescue us, we want you as king to know that we will not serve your god or worship the gold statue you set up."*
Daniel 3:1-18, emphasis added

At that moment in time, as the hulking statue of gold bore down on them from across the plain of Dura, those three Hebrew men did not know if God was going to deliver them from the horrible fate of being burned alive in the fiery furnace. They had obviously come to terms with the eventuality He might not spare them, embracing uncertainty as a necessary element to real and living faith—faith so spectacularly alive they also entertained the thought that God *would* deliver them.

That Mother's Day night, as I wrestled with hopelessness and despair, facedown before the one true and living God, I began to see that uncertainty, and even doubt, did not exclude the possibility of believing God was able to deliver me.

In his bestselling novel *The Life of Pi,* Yann Martel wrote:

If Christ spent an anguished night in prayer, if He burst out from the Cross, "My God, my God, why have you forsaken me?" then surely we are also permitted doubt. But we must move on. To choose doubt as a philosophy of life is akin to choosing immobility as a means of transportation.

As my gasping breaths of sorrow subsided, a prayer I once read, written by the monk Thomas Merton, started turning in my mind:

My Lord God, I have no idea where I am going. I do not see the road ahead of me. I cannot know for certain where it will end. Nor do I really know myself, and the fact that I think I am following your will does not mean that I am actually doing so. But I believe that the desire to please you does in fact please you. And I hope I have that desire in all that I am doing. I hope that I will never do anything apart from that desire. And I know that if I do this you will lead me by the right road, though I may know nothing about it. Therefore I will trust you always though

I may seem to be lost and in the shadow of death. I will not fear, for you are ever with me, and you will never leave me to face my perils alone.

"The desire to please you does in fact please you. . . . I hope that I will never do anything apart from that desire. And I know that if I do this you will lead me by the right road though I may know nothing about it. . . ." I shook my head as I contemplated those words. They were so simple. So profound. So unnerving. I had always believed I needed to try harder. To have a plan of action and stick to it. I had to want to experience victory. I had never once entertained I would know nothing about the right road to victory. Could that have possibly been why trying harder was so fruitless? It was impossible to try harder to arrive somewhere when I didn't even know where I was going.

As the words of the prayer continued to echo in my mind, they resonated in my heart, beat by weary beat. *"The desire to please you does in fact please you. . . ."* My heart had been so heavy, battered, and bruised for such a long time it was nearly impossible to recognize any emotions apart from shame and anger. But the words Thomas Merton wrote struck something deep within the fortress of my heart.

"I hope that I will never do anything apart from that desire. . . ." My heart started beating wildly; reverberating words and phrases were shaking the usurper's scales from my eyes. As they drifted dead, dry, and powerless to the ground, I saw truth alight before me.

"And I know that if I do this you will lead me by the right road though I may know nothing about it. . . ." I had been looking at the road ahead to victory the wrong way my entire life. Victory didn't elude me because I didn't want it badly enough. My health wasn't being restored because I didn't have the right plan.

Victory over the usurper was ever out of reach because I wanted victory **on my own terms.** I wanted to be able to see the end of the road from where I was at the beginning of it. I wanted God to reach down and miraculously deliver me. I wanted someone to tell me how to be free. I wanted someone to tell me how to do it. I wanted the strength to be able to stick to the road to victory. I wanted the ability to be able to carry it out. I wanted, I wanted, I wanted . . .

I needed to radically redefine what it was that I wanted.

I needed to redefine what wanting even was.

THE QUESTIONS TO START THE OVERTHROW

It would be very irresponsible and misleading of me to bring you this far along in my story, which truly does end in victory, and not share how I toppled the usurper. Going into treatment did not fix me. (Oh, how I wish I could say it did). However, it was the first stone in the avalanche of freedom that was to follow, because day by day, including that dark Mother's Day, I began to understand some very important things. I understood I did not need to focus my effort on knowing what the road ahead looked like. I needed to focus on Jesus. He was the road. My desire to please Him put me on the path to victory because He is the path, He is "the Way, the Truth, and the Life." When I finally let go of *my* narrow definition of victory, I discovered the battle ahead was no longer about finding the path, but staying on it.

What follows are six questions that keep me on the path, step by step, to daily victory in Jesus Christ. In moments of doubt and relapse, I return time and again to these same questions. Wrestling with and answering these questions give me both a place to begin and a place to end in my fight against the usurper because the questions are introspective and, at the same time, wholly revolutionary.

These are my six questions to being victorious:

1. Have I identified and declared war against the enemy?
2. Could I be happy if I never lost another pound or could never alter my physical appearance in any way?
3. Am I looking at the mirror inside as much as I am looking at the mirror outside?
4. What am I doing with feelings that are too much to bear?
5. Is my goal a perfect body or a *perfected* body?
6. Am I using food the way God intended?

Before you panic, let me assure you that I will cover each of these questions in great detail in the chapters that are to come. Never fear! The questions were borne of the desire to please Him and are a direct reflection of that desire. You cannot truthfully answer these questions in any meaningful and eternally satisfying way apart from that desire. Therefore, if you relentlessly and honestly wrestle with and answer these questions, you *will* discover how to overthrow the usurper.

Maybe you have leafed through the chapters of this book looking for my "thirty days to healthy eating" plan. Or maybe you've searched the pages for my new and improved exercise regimen. This is a book about disordered eating, after all! Wouldn't it make sense to include tips for physically healthy living?

The shelves are already full of such resources without me lending my voice to the cacophony of experts and entrepreneurs. There is nothing inherently wrong with these resources. You could easily choose a plan that best suits you and, if you stuck to it, would lose weight and get in shape. Again, there is nothing fundamentally wrong with this. Following Couch to 5K isn't evil. It can be a very helpful tool in helping you restore your health. It will, however, become something destructive if following the latest diet or exercise fad usurps the purpose of God in your life.

I have not been called to present a new nutritional plan. I have not been called to showcase an exercise routine. I have not been called to come up with a new, clever dietary revelation that will help you lose those pesky pounds that have been making your life miserable. I have been called to share a great truth that possibly has never been more eloquently worded than by brilliant apologist Ravi Zacharias: "Jesus did not come to make bad people good. He came to make dead people alive."

In every way and in every part of who you are, Jesus came to give you life.

I discovered the most effective way to obtain this life and find the road ahead, "though I may know nothing about it," is in the fanatical passion by which I answer those questions—the passion by which I practice the questions. Practicing answering the questions is vitally important in overthrowing the usurper. Practice makes perfect.

INTERMEDIATE BEETHOVEN

When I arrived in treatment in November 2009, I had a basic knowledge of how to play the piano, notes and chords, but nothing more. I had a piano back home that certainly wasn't "grand." It suffered from the unfortunate condition of only having one octave in tune. The keys were not what one would consider "white," and they bore the sticky residue from past attempts to identify the names of the keys with masking tape. In my own personal piano's defense, it was a hand-me-down, generously given to me by a friend, who knew that I wanted to try to teach myself to play the piano. Emphasis on the words try and teach myself. I had conquered the world of chords and was moderately able to play songs using these chords, but it was jarring. The music never seemed to flow the way it should. I vaguely knew how to read written music, but the thought of actually being able to sit down and play real songs, musical works of art composed by the likes of Beethoven, was an impossible dream.

There was a grand piano in the middle of the main room at the treatment facility. Amid dated wood paneling, brown couches littered with mismatched pillows, clusters of round tables, and medical devices, it was magnificently out of place. It was a therapeutic tool, placed there to give the women confined to that room a chance to distract themselves from the crushing reality of an eating disorder. It was a truly arresting sight: that gleaming instrument, a work of art, sitting there, surrounded by the ugliness of starvation, feeding tubes, and hopeless faces.

I was drawn to the sight of that piano from the very first moment I stepped foot in the treatment center. I was also painfully aware that, though I desperately wanted to play this gorgeous, piano, if I did indeed attempt to play it, my own feeble musical abilities would be found wanting.

It was an instrument for prodigies, I told myself. It was for people who played Mozart and Rachmaninoff by the age of six, performing in prestigious concert halls before impeccably dressed people. It was an instrument for others, for those who could play complex melodies and haunting refrains, *Moonlight Sonata* in musical perfection.

It wasn't for me. That was the one thing of which I was absolutely certain. And yet, in the middle of the treatment center, in the middle of the darkest hours of my existence, in the middle of all my wretched shame, was that grand piano. I had to walk past it every day; every activity of daily life at the treatment center was reached by way of passing the piano. Some days, I would fix my gaze straight ahead, determined not to look at it. Some days, I would allow myself to steal a furtive glance, overcome with longing. Longing began to take root, and as it grew, a thought pierced through the fog of rage and humiliation that had settled in my brain: *What would happen if you would sit down and actually try to play that beautiful grand piano?*

As days passed, marching to an agonizing rhythm, that one thought beat incessantly in my mind; I needed to know what would happen if I would allow myself to attempt to play that piano.

I had to find out.

During a sleepy afternoon slump, just after lunch, when most of the inhabitants of the treatment center were preoccupied with covering themselves with piles of pillows in preparation for a nap, I decided to find out. I sat down at the piano. After spending what seemed like hours looking at the assortment of music books arrayed on the piano, I selected *Intermediate Beethoven,* which contained *Moonlight Sonata.*

I opened the book and smoothed the page flat. I sat there.

I sat there staring at the page, my eyes burning with tears, the notes melting and blurring together on the page in front of me. Pathetic and shameful. Incompetent and unworthy. Pitiful wretch. What was I thinking? Under what monumental delusion had I been living to think I could dare to play *Moonlight Sonata* on this grand piano? Ridiculous. Humiliating. Grasping. Worthless. Useless.

I started to play.

In my first attempt, I played an almost-unrecognizable version of Moonlight Sonata. It was certainly not worthy of a concert hall. Neither was the second attempt, nor the third or the fourth or the fifth. I hit plenty of wrong notes, and often the sour notes would cry out, "Loser! You can never change. You'll never get better." As I played those first halting versions of the song, I was keenly aware of the others who were watching me. What were they thinking? Were they thinking what I was thinking? That I wasn't good enough, that there were countless others who were better than me, that I was unworthy to be playing such a magnificent instrument?

In spite of all the thoughts of condemnation turning in my head, I kept playing. There was something about that grand piano that inspired me. What was it? It was honest with me; it was always there, waiting open and inviting me to try again. It didn't judge me, yet it didn't coddle me either. It compelled me to battle on through unfamiliar notes and melodies and gave me a glimpse of the beautiful vision of what it would sound like when I truly conquered that song on that instrument.

And one day I sat down at the grand piano. I played *Moonlight Sonata*. I didn't have to think about what I was doing; the music flowed from the depth of my soul, through my practiced hands, and resonated in graceful song. It was a moment of such unexpected beauty and accomplishment it nearly took my breath away. I was fully aware that I was still far away from my home and family, I was still engaged in the fight of my life, and there were thousands upon thousands of songs still left to be learned and perfected. But I recognized I had done what I had only dreamed possible: in the midst of all the very present, ongoing turmoil, I mastered a song on that magnificent instrument.

Mastery requires practice. Practice and determination. In the beginning, mastering the questions may seem like the impossible dream. Maybe you feel like you can't see how the way ahead could ever appear clear or end in victory. Maybe you feel like Shadrach, Meshach, and Abednego, and fighting the usurper, the eating disorder, feels like you are contending with the fate of the fiery furnace. How could God possibly ever be able to deliver?

But God *did* deliver Shadrach, Meshach, and Abednego. They faced down the king of Babylon, his legions of soldiers and governors and counselors, and the very fires of the blazing furnace itself. Even in the midst of uncertainty, they were confident in one thing: they would never serve the gods of Nebuchadnezzar or worship the golden statue. They could not see the road ahead, but they trusted that He would lead them by the right road, though they knew nothing about it. Though they might have felt lost and in the shadow of death, they did not fear. For He would never leave them to face their perils alone.

> And these three men, Shadrach, Meshach, and Abednego, fell, bound, into the furnace of blazing fire.
>
> Then King Nebuchadnezzar jumped up in alarm. He said to his advisers, "Didn't we throw three men, bound, into the fire?"
>
> "Yes, of course, Your Majesty," they replied to the king.
>
> He exclaimed, "Look! I see four men, not tied, walking around in the fire unharmed; and the fourth looks like the son of the gods."
> Daniel 3:23-25

Practicing answering the questions on a regular basis is how you overthrow the usurper. You practice and practice and practice. And when you tire of doing that, when thoughts of self-doubt and deprecation threaten to ruin your hard work, take a deep breath and practice some more. Practice truly does make perfect. One day you will sit down, and a beautiful song will flow from your hands in practiced grace, each note a testimony to the God who never left you to face your perils alone.

I would like to offer this word of encouragement to you. Last Mother's Day, my oldest daughter handed me a card. I was genuinely surprised by the gesture. I hadn't been expecting anything because we were at a volleyball tournament in a different state, where she was playing and I was coaching. My eyes filled with tears as I read the words she had written in the card:

I'll never find better footsteps to follow than yours, Mom.
Happy Mother's Day! I'm so glad I get to spend it with you.
Thank you for everything you do for me and always being there for
me—in good times and bad. You're my role model. I love you.

Amazement is too poor a word to describe how I felt as I read the words she wrote . . . to me . . . her mother. My soul rang with joy as I looked back and realized how far I had come from that Mother's Day spent sobbing at the altar. My daughter's beautiful handwriting lovingly penned across the card proved it.

Freedom really is possible.

CHAPTER 10

War

Hence the saying: If you know the enemy and you know yourself,
you need not fear the result of a hundred battles.

THE ART OF WAR, SUN TZÚ

QUESTION 1: Have I Identified and Declared War Against the Enemy?

Here we are at the threshold of the questions I have been alluding to so doggedly. I have split them up in sections of thought that felt the most natural to me. As I described in the previous chapter, I began coming up with these questions in response to the organic progression of my own fight and my own victory. I pursued the desire to please Him and that desire brought me to this threshold and brought me to these questions. I truly do practice answering these questions in my own life. Every day. These questions are also beginning and ending points along the timeline of this life we all follow. They are designed to be thought provokers, not multiple choice questions on some kind of cosmic test. With all of that in mind, we forge ahead; for He will show us the right road, "though we may know nothing about it."

Do you want victory over the usurper, over your flesh, over the desires that war against the Spirit, over the part of you that is constantly striving to find fulfillment apart from the love and the mercy of God? Do you feel a battle cry rising in your spirit to stand and fight? Are you making a decision *right now* that you are willing to do whatever it takes to win? Are you ready to make war and rattle the gates of the enemy?

You have decided you want to fight. But how does one start a war?

I would submit in order to start a war, the most preliminary act is to **IDENTIFY THE ENEMY**.

Identifying the enemy is simply this: separating your identity from the identity of the usurper. You are not the eating disorder. You are not your struggle with food. You are no longer a victim of shame and regret. You are not collateral damage in someone else's dysfunctional destruction. You are not a pitiful mistake. You are not too far away from the reaches of redemption.

The usurper, your flesh, the eating disorder, is the enemy.

You are not the enemy.

And you are worth fighting for.

After identifying the enemy, the second act of starting a war, of bringing it front and center to your active, conscious self, is to **DECLARE WAR**.

How can one possibly fight and win a war if war is not declared in the first place? The United States' involvement in the Vietnam War is a very good example. It was never actually declared a war; it was termed a "strategic military engagement." After all the fighting and sacrifice and blood and sweat and agony, it was never called what it really was. What victory could ever be definitively quantified, no matter how hard fought, from a strategic military engagement?

When you declare war, you are announcing your intention to fight, to see it through to the end, and to dedicate every resource you possess to achieve victory. You must declare war against the usurper. Victory can only be found on the other side of war.

How do you declare war?

Tell someone.

You must tell someone you are struggling. Tell them what you struggle with. And believe me when I say I understand the enormity of what I am asking you to do.

The moment I decided to declare war and tell someone happened on an ordinary day in October. It was a clear day; an abundance of red and golden leaves had swirled and danced in the chilly wind. But day was fading to night . . . slowly fading. Lingering colors suspended in the western sky turned to a comforting gray. This had always been my favorite time of day, the tranquil time just before dusk. The day was spent and gave a contented sigh. The sigh could be seen in the gilded edges of the clouds and felt in the evening's cool breath. In that moment, I did not appreciate the grandeur of the twilight; I did not breathe deeply of the air that smelled heavier with the perfume of almost night; I did not notice the tiny points of light that were beginning to appear in the darkening sky, the solemn glow of the moon as it lifted its face to illuminate the somber earth.

I felt like I was going to die. I had been acting out in my eating disorder in every unimaginable way for months and months and months. My body was spent, my mind was ravaged, and I was at a true breaking point.

There were two choices before me that day: One, give up and end it all. I would cut the ties that bound me to this life. I knew I would leave a trail of destruction and shattered lives behind me, but I was weary and the dark was fast approaching. Or two, give up and cry out for help. I simply could not do this by myself any longer. This point in my life could be described as the bottom. It was the reaching of some limit, although I had felt that I had reached the precipice of what I could bear countless times before. And yet, in a twisted, grotesque mockery of the human spirit, I had somehow managed to keep going, always wondering how bad it really had to get in order for it to indeed be the end of all things.

I sat alone in a room, with the darkness of the night shadows seeping in through the windows and doors. I felt as though I was no longer a part of myself, like I was watching a suffocating blackness envelope someone I used to know, someone I hadn't seen or heard from for so long I was completely detached from her.

As I sat there, I felt like the preferable course of action was to keep watching that person I used to know become swallowed in complete darkness and never think of her again. That would be the best for everyone; that would be the easiest. Yes, I decided, I would indeed go gently into that good night. I just couldn't resolve myself to think tomorrow, tomorrow, tomorrow one more exhausting time. Maybe somehow I could will myself into nothingness. Maybe God would be merciful. Surely God, who knows all things, would understand that in the end, I had no choice but to succumb to this wretched existence.

In solitary confinement I sat, with death before me. I just had to muster the strength to will myself to one last action.

A light came on. I could see it illuminating the edges of the door. Why did someone have to turn on a light? I thought miserably. I had finally come to the decision that the eating disorder had been preparing me to make for the last two decades. I knew that if I didn't keep watching the woman in the darkness, I would lose control. If I responded to the light, I would break. And being out of control and broken were completely unacceptable. Light flooded in, overwhelming the darkness as the door swung open. My husband stood in the doorway.

"Why are you sitting alone in the dark?" he asked.

It was a perfectly reasonable question to ask of someone who was sitting alone in a dark room. A reasonable question to which I had no response. I watched the woman, the woman I think I used to know, hang her head and begin to cry. She seemed to have lost the power of sound and of speech. I watched her shoulders shaking in silence, each breath a shuddering sob that seemed to rattle every part of her and yet produced no noise at all. And then I watched as she got up, staggered across the room, and fell into her husband's arms.

There, in his arms, I could no longer see that woman, because once again I was that woman, and I heard a cracking noise, like a gunshot, like ice breaking on a frozen lake, as everything I had every known before broke apart.

"I am powerless and my life is unmanageable. Help me—I'll do anything!"

Did I really just say that? Did I really mean that? What did it mean to *do anything?* My husband looked at me. There was weariness in his eyes, and worry and fear. And yes, anger, too. But there was also love; its edges were worn away, but it was still there.

Out of love my husband orchestrated a plan of action for my treatment. I realize now that he violently seized what could have possibly been his last chance to help me. One last chance to save me. And he was going to do everything in his power to make sure I really got the help I needed. Not just the help I thought I wanted.

He researched treatment facilities and showed them to me. As I looked them over with desperation and a creeping sensation of disdain, I felt myself slipping away again. But I had agreed to this, and I knew that this time if I didn't follow through, my marriage was over. So I chose one. I chose a date to enter, November 9. Just another ordinary day and the end of the world to me.

Indeed, I was the one doing the choosing, but it felt like I was choosing those things for someone else. It was as if I were listening to someone else's testimony or reading the story of someone else's life. I would think thoughts like, *Isn't it sad what is happening to that poor woman. But hopefully it will all work out in the end.* Or, *I can't believe she is telling the pastor and his wife what is going on. Look at that—they are crying! It looks like they care about her.*

The time period between when I fell into my husband's arms and when I actually got off the plane in Phoenix to enter the inpatient treatment facility seemed like an out-of-body experience. The climax of that out-of-body sensation happened on a Sunday morning, before an entire congregation of Sunday morning churchgoers.

As part of the unfolding plan for my regeneration, I was required to let the congregants know the reason for my sudden and lengthy departure. My brain understood this was necessary, because it really wasn't fair for me to just disappear, leaving my husband and children to cover for my mysterious whereabouts. But my brain and my body were not coexisting during this time of my life, so I found myself floating above someone dressed in her Sunday best on November 8. She was standing alone on a hard, unforgiving platform, flanked by faux marble pillars, a piano, and a wooden throne, clutching a microphone as a lifeline, the only thing tethering her to the stage.

Shame was palpable in that place; it was closing in on her as she started to explain what was wrong with her, what she was unable to do, how she was unable to help herself. I listened as she explained what an eating disorder was, why it was so dangerous, and how hard of a choice going into treatment really was. I watched as she shrank down in complete openness and vulnerability.

And then . . .

I saw Jesus. He was hanging on a cross, and the light of the sun was obscured with unnatural darkness. He was tortured and exposed, the King of the Jews, humbled to death, even death on a cross. The earth shook so violently that even the rocks broke apart. It was finished.

I saw Jesus, as He was on that Good/Bad Friday. There He was, and I was finally identified with Him and He with me. We were together.

A thought seized me with thunderous force, and I was no longer merely a spectator. I was fully aware. Hadn't Jesus made Himself completely vulnerable when He hung naked and dying on the cross for my guilt, my secrets, and my shame? This was the way of the cross, the way of redemption.

That day, before my harshest critics and most fervent supporters, I shone a light on my shame, a spotlight on what I thought condemned me to the farthest corners of failure. Make no mistake—I wasn't instantly healed and carried off on rapturous clouds of glory. Yet something changed. Deception withered beneath the scorching light of truth. Not just the truth of what Jesus had done for me, but the whole truth—who I really was: the good, the bad, and the desperately ugly.

I walked off the platform, my mind buzzing with electricity. The shock of what I had just done was sending pulses of energy to my spirit. I had done it . . . I had gone through with it. What I had thought would be the ruination of everything I valued in my life had turned into something altogether different. It had turned into determination. Determination to cling to the vision of the crucified Christ, allowing my fellowship with His suffering to be the guiding star illuminating the way to victory on the other side. I certainly didn't have a clue what was going to come next. It was enough in that moment to know that my husband had opened a door and flooded the dark room I was in with light. He met me where I was. Christ had done the same; He had flooded my soul with determination to count the cost of Good Friday, the saddest day the earth has ever known, filled with vulnerability and sorrow. A determination to see the incalculable, redemptive value of pain. A determination to work through the days ahead . . . no matter what was to come . . . for resurrection was waiting on the other side.

Now, you certainly don't have to stand up in a public forum and announce your many failings like a town crier bent on self-destruction. Just find someone who is safe. Make certain you can be assured what you tell them will be kept in strict confidence, until you are ready to let others know. That is how you **declare war.** Once you have **declared war,** you will find that it is really a declaration of determination. And determination is not an emotion; it is decisive action despite of, and in spite of, emotion.

Take courage, fellow soldier, and "Be very glad—for these trials make you partners with Christ in his suffering, so that you will have the wonderful joy of seeing his glory when it is revealed to all the world" (1 Peter 4:13, nlt).

CHAPTER 11

The Definition of Happiness

If you stumble at mere believability, what are you living for? . . .
Love is hard to believe, ask any lover. Life is hard to believe,
ask any scientist. God is hard to believe, ask any believer.
What is your problem with hard to believe?

"LIFE OF PI," YANN MARTEL

QUESTION 2: Could I Be Happy If I Never Lost Another Pound
or Could Never Alter My Physical Appearance in Any Way?

Up to this point I have been endeavoring to tell you something
about me—who I am, who I have been, the lies I have believed
and the choices I have made. I have attempted to convey a life that
crumbled beneath the weight of shame and condemnation. I have
labored to share all of this with you in the hope that you could
perhaps see yourself, or a part of yourself, in my story. Or perhaps
gain understanding and a new perspective on food issues and the
complexity of eating disorders and disordered eating.

I have shared my life with you to prove to you that I know what
it means to fight. I have fought to the brink of death. I made a decision, a determination, standing on a platform in front of a church,
in the face of complete despair, to fight the usurper with everything

I possessed. I **declared war,** pledging to spend the rest of my life in violent combat against my flesh. I vowed that I would never stop pursuing victory. . . . As Winston Churchill famously said, I wanted *"victory at all costs, victory in spite of all terror, victory, however long and hard the road may be; for without victory, there is no survival."*

If I could wave a magic wand, and in the blink of an eye, you could be free from the tyranny of the flesh and the chains of the eating disorder, would you want me to do it? No more fighting, no more war. Just instantaneous deliverance. Take a moment and close your eyes. I want you to paint a picture in your mind. Visualize the grand and glorious moment, when with a burst of dazzling light, every issue you have ever had with food is swallowed up in victory. All the struggle and the heartache vanish into thin air.

You are free.

Take a deep breath.

What does victory look like?

Can you see it? What are you feeling?

Are you happy? Are you content? Are you fulfilled?

Perhaps you are exclaiming, "Yes! I can see it! That is what I want . . . to be finally free and happy! All I have ever wanted was to be happy!"

Ask yourself one more question: what does that free, happy, delivered person look like?

In your vision of "the end," the moment you were finally, once and for all, forever free, what did you look like? Be honest. Be brutally honest. Visualize your liberated self. Picture the image of the person that you long to be, when all is said and done and victory from the usurper is finally yours.

I would venture to say that if we were being truthful, we all envisioned a similar version of the same thing: a thin person. A person who wakes up in the morning and gets dressed, easily fitting into beautiful clothes, confidently buttoning them, zipping them, slipping into them. Never a troubled thought. *Will it fit the same way today?* Never a shadow of fear. *What if it doesn't fit the same way?* The mirror is a friend, not an adversary.

With that image in mind, take one more moment; I want you to allow yourself one more searching look inside your vision of the "end." Imagine that you are released at long last from the slavery of shame and the usurper . . . and you look exactly as you do now. You haven't lost a blessed pound; your physical appearance has not changed one iota. Ask yourself this question: **"If I never lost another pound, or could never alter my physical appearance in any way, could I be truly happy?"**

I asked myself that question for decades, and truthfully, my answer was always a resounding "No!" (Actually, it would have been a four-letter word—_ _ _ _ *no!*) I had always been afraid that when I finally was free of the usurper, I would gain weight. And lots of it. Maybe I would be free of the eating disorder, but I would have exchanged one shameful condition for another.

Hadn't I always believed that thinness equals happiness? It was impossible to extricate one of those elusive ideas from the other. They orbited around my shameful existence; I felt the constant pull of their gravity. But they were as far away as the moon, as unreachable as Pluto. Happiness and thinness were the carrot constantly dangled before my face, spurring me on to take the next step only to find that I was still one step behind. Always one step behind. My life had been lived in an endless vigil anticipating the arrival of thinness, which would bring with it the arrival of happiness.

How could I have possibly ever hoped to be free and happy if I could never lose another pound? I had to honestly admit to myself that while I desperately wanted freedom, I was unwilling to accept freedom on the condition I could never lose another pound. *I didn't want freedom on those terms. I wanted it on mine.*

Theologian Blaise Pascal wrote about this idea of wanting freedom, happiness, on our own terms:

All men seek happiness. This is without exception. Whatever different means they employ, they all tend to this end. The cause of some going to war, and of others avoiding it, is the same desire in both, attended with different views. The will never takes the least step but to this object. This is the motive of every action of every man, even of those who hang themselves.

What does happiness look like? Is it thin? Does it wear a particular size? Does enduring joy weigh a certain amount? Is it always well-groomed and put together?

The truth is, real happiness is a mess. It is a romp in the mud. It is a father scooping his mud-covered child up in his arms and holding her close. It is a table covered with crayons, the box of 101 colors knocked on its side by the zealous artist, intent on her masterpiece. It is the sticky fingers of a little girl grasping her mother's hand. It is sand-covered, sunburned *everything* after a day at the seashore. It is a cup of spilled juice, with a comforting hug and a promise "we will clean this up together." It is the Good Shepherd leaving ninety-nine obedient sheep He already gathered safely in the shelter to find the one who wandered and got lost, rescuing it from the clutches of a thicket. It is a lover, spinning his beloved on the dance floor, two left feet and all, for the joy her company. It is a closet of too-small clothes from which there is now no condemnation.

I am not a therapist. I've never been to seminary. But I have researched, and I have studied, and I have experienced the hell that is an imprisonment to an eating disorder, and I have tried *everything* in an attempt to find true contentment. To find true happiness.

From cognitive behavioral therapy to exorcism—I looked into

it all. I tried meals plans, intuitive eating, and nutritional supplements. I exercised—Pilates, yoga, cardio, slow walks on the beach, long hikes in the mountains, running, DVD workouts, fitness club memberships. I ate a Levitical diet—if it was good enough for Moses, it was good enough for me! I enrolled in classes to obtain a degree in holistic medicine and read book after book about how to eat in the cleanest way possible. I attempted to find lasting recovery in eating very healthfully and exercising moderately. (My body is a temple, right?) I focused solely on health goals and got rid of the scale. I practiced positive self-talk. I took handfuls of vitamins and drank shaker cups of nutritionally balanced plant-based smoothies. I volunteered to speak about self-esteem to teenage girls. I went to a therapist and kept a journal, chronicling the food choices I made and the emotions I felt while I was making them. I tried cleanses, believing maybe something was chemically unbalanced within me and could be corrected with proper food choices.

You name it—I probably tried it. I left no stone unturned in my quest to search out true happiness. I am not ashamed of this. In *The Hobbit,* J. R. R. Tolkien described the process of discovery in which I was engaged: "There is nothing like looking, if you want to find something. . . . You certainly usually find something, if you look, but it is not always quite the something you were after."

I am proud of my looking because I demonstrated to myself and to those around me that I really wanted to recover. I was willing to do whatever it took to do so. I am also very thankful I tried everything I did because I came to realize that the means and methods by which I had been seeking to find happiness did indeed have some value. Eating healthfully and exercising moderately certainly didn't hurt my physical body. Good nutrition is a positive thing. Likewise, holistic medicine and positive self-talk are not bad things. They can be very helpful tools in managing my physical body.

But what if I told you these interventions never have had in the past, and never will have in the future, no matter how clever, cutting edge, or innovative, any lasting power to make a meaningful difference in the life of an eternal soul? What if I told you that the breaking of chains and the gaining of permanent, lasting freedom has absolutely nothing whatsoever to do with food, your body, or anything that "moth nor rust destroys" (Matthew 6:20)?

You see, what I know, and I bet you know it, too, is that true and lasting transformation is only possible when it happens from the inside out. True and lasting happiness can only be found when it is anchored in something that can never be taken away. Putting into practice the very best the world had to offer did at times lead to my improved physical health. However, what each of these journeys proved was that the world was exceptionally good at promising happiness and freedom and incapable of actually delivering on it. I was no closer to transformative victory than when I had begun. Honestly, in moments like those, I began to doubt victory was even possible. Facing that disillusionment persuaded me I had been sold a bill of goods. I had been the unwilling and eager victim of the classic bait-and-switch scam.

I felt betrayed.

BETRAYAL RUNS DEEP

I don't have the best track record when it comes to celebrating Thanksgiving. The Thanksgiving I attempted to run away from the treatment center certainly was the pinnacle of my dysfunctional holiday experiences, but even prior to that dark day, Thanksgiving had always been a dreaded occasion. It involved the expectation of consuming large quantities of food and smiling while I was forced to do so. It was a time when we would travel, usually halfway across the country, to spend the holiday with family. Travel in and of itself was problematic because it was fraught with many variables and unknowns that I could not control. It also required being around people, when isolation was my preferred method of existence.

Invariably, my husband would become angry with me. He simply could not understand why I would choose to behave in such an irrational manner at a time we were supposed to be thankful and content. Without fail, we would spend the blessed time around the table in stony silence.

Christmas and Halloween were close seconds, but Thanksgiving held the place of preeminence on my list of most hated days of the year. I couldn't fathom ever feeling differently. The blare of the football game on the television, the peals of laughter, the smells of food, so enticing and so damning, all reinforced that I was living in a place that was not quite a part of the land of the living. It wasn't the land of the dead . . . not yet. But I felt closer to death than life during those days. With every forkful of food I was obligated to pretend to enjoy eating, I became more and more set apart from life. Life that everyone else seemed to live so effortlessly.

I have a very distinct memory of the Thanksgiving *before* I decided to go into treatment. I remember it well because I hosted it at my house. My stomach was knotted with dread as I carefully arranged each place setting on the red-painted dining table. Plate in the center, fork to the left on a folded napkin, knife and spoon to the right, blade facing the plate. I felt as if I were fashioning a monument to the unholy event to come. I knew it wasn't right, feeling that way. I longed for it to be different: to set a table with love, for the joy of the occasion, not in slavery to the calculations of my mind.

Anemic rays of sunlight were coming in through the windows, casting faded square-shaped patterns on the table, over the place settings. I stopped what I was doing and stared at them. Even the sunshine was struggling for survival. It was trying its best to shine with warmth and happiness but was failing, subjected to the reality of a gray November day. The light felt cold and far away. All of a sudden, a different kind of thought broke through my melancholy reverie with the force of a freight train.

What if?

What if it did not have to be this way? What if it were really possible for me to participate in a Thanksgiving meal and remember it fondly? What if I could look back on this day and recollect the way the freckles spread across my daughter's tiny nose and how her eyes shone when she smiled, instead of how tight I was sure my clothes would become? What if I could understand, really and truly understand, that I would never pass that way again? The pale, November sunlight would never move across that red-painted table in the same way again.

I remember the reckless, captivating thought of *"What if?"* so clearly because I remember with exacting detail what happened right after. My hopeful sentiments were enough to carry me through the meal. However, in a moment of panic, I excused myself from the table and the usurper reminded me that hope was for fools. Hope was for people who were free. Hope was not for slaves.

The betrayal of my flesh, the usurper, ran deep. It had promised me so much. It had promised me so much and delivered *nothing*. I had spent years believing that if I could just make it through to the next day, then tomorrow would be the day the usurper finally delivered on what it had been promising. But as the rising of each new day's sun brought with it only disappointment, hope began to feel like a fairy tale: a lovely story that couldn't possibly be true.

I know full well what it feels like to offer up your battered hope for the promise of freedom, only to be bitterly frustrated. You can believe me when I say I understand the magnitude of what I am asking you to imagine . . . a life where you could be happy if you never lost another pound or could alter your physical appearance in any way. A life built on the unbelievable promise of hope.

Truly, it is only when we begin to fight against the usurper with all of our might that we are finally able to see the extent of the treachery. With each victory, as we reclaim territory previously held by the enemy, we are finally able to see that what it had been telling us all those years was untrue. It constructed a vast labyrinth of lies. Breaking through those lies is no easy task. It takes time and unwavering resolve.

That is why this second question I pose to you is vitally important: **Could you be happy if you never lost another pound or could never alter your physical appearance in any way?** The moment you can answer yes and mean it from the depths of your soul, you have torn down one of the usurper's greatest lies.

The Lie: I can be free, but my happiness is still anchored in my physical appearance. It is anchored in something that can change.

The Truth: I can be free, and my happiness is anchored in something that can never be taken away. It is anchored in something that will never change—eternal hope found in Jesus Christ.

Dietrich Bonhoeffer wrote, *"Jesus is the only significance. Beside Jesus nothing has significance. He alone matters."* 1 Timothy 4:8 tells us, "the training of the body has a limited benefit, but godliness is beneficial in every way, since it holds promise for the present life and also for the life to come." (nlt)

Eternal perspective changes everything. It enables us to see and understand that which is "beneficial in every way." The truth that I am not a physical being, but rather, a spiritual being having a brief and momentary physical experience is a liberating and happy truth, indeed. When we anchor our freedom to Jesus, and the hope of eternal life, we are not only anchoring our happiness to something that can never change or be taken away, we are anchoring ourselves to happiness itself.

"The kingdom of heaven is like a treasure buried in a field, that a man found and reburied. Then in his joy he goes and sells everything he has and buys that field. Again, the kingdom of heaven is like a merchant in search of fine pearls. When he found one priceless pearl, he went and sold everything he had, and bought it" (Matthew 13:44-45).

When we, as Stephen Covey wrote, "begin with the end in mind," we set our sights on the goal of a freedom and a happiness that can never be stripped away. We fix our eyes on "the end," a victorious Kingdom that can never be shaken.

Where we want to end up makes all the difference in the world. Lewis Carroll wrote about a little girl named Alice. Shortly after falling down a rabbit hole into Wonderland, she encountered a Cheshire Cat, sitting on the bough of a tree. She had never been in Wonderland before. Alice asked the Cat, "'Would you tell me please, which way I ought to go from here?'

'That depends a good deal on where you want to get to,' said the Cat..

'I don't much care where,' said Alice.

'Then it doesn't much matter which way you go,' said the Cat.

If we don't know where we want to end up going, any road will do. We will be as leaves, waiting for the wind to blow us in the right direction. But the problem is, any wind can blow.

Ask yourself one last time, "Could I be happy if I never lost another pound or could never alter my physical appearance any way?"

Maybe it is impossible for you to imagine a life without the tyranny of needing to be a certain size to feel that you have value. That's okay. Because we are going to begin to fight together with the end in mind. Picture the end. And the end isn't what we always dreamed our appearance would be.

It is Jesus. Picture Jesus.

"For consider Him who endured such hostility from sinners against Himself, so that you won't grow weary and lose heart" (Hebrews 12:3). Consider Him, the first and the last, the beginning and end.

We are going to keep seeking and looking, understanding that the methods we may try in order to overcome the eating disorder are means to an end, not ends to themselves.

In *The Cost of Discipleship,* Bonhoeffer also wrote, "When all is said and done, the life of faith is nothing if not *an unending struggle of the Spirit with every available weapon against the flesh"*—in other words, this is a fight. A bloody, bare-knuckle fight to the finish.

Yes, there will be many days filled with toiling and striving in pursuit of the promise of victory. Winston Churchill said in his legendary victory speech, "I have nothing to offer but blood, toil, tears, and sweat." Anything that is really worth having is worth fighting for. And a life of faith is worth fighting for because in the purest sense possible, at its heart, a life of faith is a life of hope.

> Now in this hope we were saved, yet hope that is seen is not hope, because who hopes for what he sees? But if we hope for what we do not see, we eagerly wait for it with patience.
> Romans 8:24-25

Hope that Thanksgiving does not have to be a lamentable occasion.

This past year, I had Thanksgiving at my house yet again. I remember preparing food with my daughter, noticing how freckles spread across her tiny nose and how her eyes shone when she smiled. I remember a table set with love, brimming with delicious things to eat. I remember stacks and stacks and stacks of dishes to be washed, piled in wanton disarray all over the counter. I remember deciding that washing the dishes could wait because at that moment the sun was setting, a fiery banner of pink-and-golden flame suspended across the darkening sky. I remember my husband was smiling, laughing even. What once had been lost was now found.

War is worth fighting because freedom is worth having. So fight! We begin to fight, with the eternal end in our hearts and our minds so that in the darkest hour, when the usurper peddles its treachery once more, you will not be persuaded to give up.

In *The Two Towers,* Tolkien wrote, "War must be, while we defend our lives against a destroyer who would devour all; but I do not love the bright sword for its sharpness, nor the arrow for its swiftness, nor the warrior for his glory. I love only that which they defend."

Thanksgiving is worth defending.

So fight!

CHAPTER 12

Mirror, Mirror

*If you want to build a ship, don't drum up the men
to gather wood, decide the work, and give orders. Instead,
teach them to yearn for the vast and endless sea . . .*

ATTRIBUTED TO ANTOINE DE SAINT-EXUPERY

QUESTION 3: Am I Looking at the Mirror
Inside as Much as the Mirror Outside?

The mirror is an inanimate object.

Despite childhood tales of "Magic mirror, on the wall, who is the fairest one of all?" and Alice falling through the looking glass, the mirror itself does not possess any magical power. It does not have the power to transport you to a world of wonders unknown, nor does it search the face of the earth to ascertain which inhabitant possesses the most beauty.

The mirror is an amoral object. It is perfectly neutral in its morality. Despite what you have been told, by other people or by yourself, the reflection in the mirror is neither good nor bad. It is neither benevolent, nor is it evil. It just *is*.

Yet despite this truth, the mirror is nonetheless a fearsome thing to face. When we look in the mirror, we want it to reveal something to us. We might look at the mirror through a prism of hope, wanting it to give us confidence, pride in our self-control, confirmation that our bodies are cooperating with us for the time being. We seek a revelation of happiness. Or, conversely, we might look at the mirror through a lens of dread. We expect to see the worst in ourselves. We want the mirror to tell us that what we fear is true: we really are a walking representation of gluttony and ugliness. A revelation of shame.

But as mirrors really are inanimate and amoral objects, they are incapable of giving us what we are seeking. They have nothing to offer in the way of truth. The only thing mirrors can offer is the ability to reflect what is put in front of them.

But what if there is another kind of mirror? A mirror made of eternal truth, which is anything but inanimate and amoral, which reflects what is *inside* a person.

THE FIRST MIRROR

The first kind of mirror has its uses. Mirrors made of glass are used in areas of scientific advancements, in solar panels and microscopes, etc. They are also utilized in other numerous and varied applications. I, for one, am glad those kinds of mirrors exist so that I can check for the errant piece of spinach in my teeth and spare others from having to endure the not-so-majestic reality of bedhead. They are useful for general hygiene and grooming. Although, strictly speaking, one could reasonably spend their whole life never once gazing into a physical mirror. (Maybe we would be the better for it. Who knows?)

There once was a fellow who did the exact opposite of never gazing into a physical mirror. The Roman poet Ovid wrote in his masterwork, *Metamorphoses,* about a young man who was the son of the river-god and a nymph named Liriope. This young man was "unequalled for his beauty." His name was Narcissus.

In Ovid's telling of this myth, Narcissus catches the eye of a noisy nymph named Echo, who notices him "wandering in the pathless woods; she loved him" and followed him, waiting for the moment she could reveal herself and capture his affection. But Echo had an obstacle to overcome before she could make her love known; she had been cursed by the goddess Juno and was not able to speak of her own free will, but rather, was only able to "mock the sounds of other's voices, or perchance, return their final words." As a result, she is forced to continue to follow him, waiting until he first speaks.

She cannot choose but wait the moment when his voice may give to her an answer.

Presently the youth [Narcissus], by chance divided from his trusted friends, cries loudly, "Who is here?" and Echo "Here!" replies. Amazed, he casts his eyes around, and calls with a louder voice, "Come here!" "Come here!" She calls the youth who calls. He turns to see who calls him, and beholding naught exclaims, "Avoid me not!" "Avoid me not!" returns.

He tries again, again, and is deceived by this alternate voice, and calls aloud; "Oh let us come together!" Echo cries, "Oh let us come together!" Never sound seemed sweeter to the Nymph, and from the woods she hastens in accordance with her words, and strives to wind her arms around his neck. He flies from her and as he leaves her says; "Take off our hands! you shall not fold your arms around me. Better death than such a one should ever caress me!" Naught she answers save, "Caress me!"

Thus rejected she lies hid in the deep woods, hiding her blushing face with the green leaves; and ever after lives concealed in lonely caverns in the hills.

But her great love increases with neglect; her miserable body wastes away, wakeful with sorrows; leanness shrivels up her skin, and all her lovely features melt, as if dissolved upon the wafting winds—nothing remains except her bones and voice—her voice continues, in the wilderness; her bones have turned to stone. She lies concealed in the wild woods, nor is she ever seen on lonely mountain range; for though we hear her calling in the hills, 'tis but a voice, a voice that lives, that lives among the hills.

Echo met a sad fate. The callousness by which she was rejected pushed her to the point she no longer had the will to live. Narcissus's complete disregard for her feelings was the deathblow to her spirit. It was Narcissus's undoing, as well. Echo's plight did not go unnoticed—the goddess Nemesis (the spirit of divine retribution against those who succumb to hubris) cursed Narcissus. "If he should love deny him what he loves!"

One day, Narcissus, "tired of hunting and the heated noon" laid down next to a "fountain silver-clear and bright . . . its waters were unsullied—birds disturbed it not; nor animals, nor boughs that fall so often from the trees." It was there, in a place of idyllic natural beauty, he "stooped to quench his thirst."

While he is drinking he beholds himself reflected in the mirrored pool—and loves; loves an imagined body which contains no substance, for he deems the mirrored shade a thing of life to love. . . . His gaze is fixed on his own eyes, twin stars. . . . All that is lovely in himself he loves, and in his witless way he wants himself: he who approves is equally approved; he seeks, is sought, he burns and is burnt.

He laid there on the gilded banks of the pool, the green, unrivaled glory of nature hemming in the edges of the crystal water, and began to understand. He understood that he was beholding something he was desperately longing for (himself); he had been longing for himself his whole life. This revelation did not bring comfort with it, for he also understood he could never possess it. Overcome with despair and grief "did he pine away, by love consumed, and slowly wasted by a hidden flame."

In the end, he died, consumed by unrequited longing. He made his choice, and in so doing he succumbed to the curse of Nemesis (The Inescapable). He decided that happiness and fulfillment could only be found in what he believed was reflected in the mirror of silver water. Acting according to that belief led him to his untimely end.

Eating disorders and issues with food are not about vanity. Truly, they are not. But we cannot ignore that while they are not about an obsession with the mirror itself, our obsession with what we believe to be reflected in the mirror has become the yardstick by which we measure success and control. The preeminence we place on what is reflected in the mirror reveals our misplaced longing to find our heart's desire. This misplaced longing gives power to our flesh. It strengthens the usurper.

I was once given a book titled *Get Over Yourself.* I understood that the intentions of the person who had given me the book were in the right place, and maybe the book could have been helpful. All the same, it was an insurmountable task for me to be able to get over the fact that someone thought my struggles could be remedied by reading a book titled *Get Over Yourself.* That was one of the prevailing diagnoses offered to me: "Just eat and get over it."

"You are so thin; just get over it."

"You look fine to me; just get over it."

"Quit whining about how overweight you are; do something about it. And get over it."

Hidden in the words *get over it* was the mantra "What a monstrously vain person you are. If you weren't so self-absorbed, you could easily get over yourself."

Whenever I would stand in front of the mirror, facing the brutality of the reflection, my belief that others viewed me as Narcissus incarnate was reinforced. I just couldn't get over what I would find there, whether I found depression or ecstasy. I would either be horrified and ashamed of what I saw, or I would be comforted, proud that I could see the outline of bones I had never seen before and overjoyed that clothes which used to fit tightly now hung loosely. The mirror delivered myself to me. But as time went on, even the moments of ecstasy were not enough to persuade me that what I longed for could be found in what I saw in the mirror. For the mirror is an inanimate and amoral object. All it can do is reflect what is put in front of it.

I was unable to believe that was true because I *needed* it to tell me who I was. I needed it to give me what I was longing for. I was willing to be "slowly wasted by a hidden flame" in front of it to find what I was so desperately seeking.

How would I know who I was if the mirror didn't tell me?

THE SECOND MIRROR

The second type of mirror stands in diametric contrast to the first one. This mirror is made of eternal truth and is designed to reflect what is *inside* a person. This mirror is called Self-Examination.

J. K. Rowling wrote about a mirror in *Harry Potter and the Sorcerer's Stone*. Harry was an eleven-year-old boy who had grown up as an orphan, never knowing his parents, always feeling entirely unloved and unwanted by the aunt and uncle who had taken him in. He had just discovered a whole magical world existed, of which he was, and had always unknowingly been, a part. To gain an education in the magical arts he needed in order to live and function in this new world, he attended Hogwarts School for Witchcraft and Wizardry. While at Hogwarts, during a rule-breaking, nighttime wandering through the castle, he stumbled upon a "magnificent mirror, as high as the ceiling, with an ornate gold frame, standing on two clawed feet."

When Harry looked in the mirror, he was shocked to see not only himself, but for the first time in his life, his whole family crowded around him in his reflection. He had never known his parents—he could hardly believe his eyes that they were there, in the mirror, smiling at him. Since there was much about the world of magic he did not understand, his thoughts raced: Could his parents actually be inside the mirror?

The wise headmaster, Professor Dumbledore, noticed Harry returning night after night, to sit in front of the mirror, gazing at his family with desperate longing. He explained to Harry that his parents were not inside the mirror.

"Let me explain. The happiest man on earth would be able to use the Mirror of Erised like a normal mirror, that is, he would look into it and see himself exactly as he is. Does that help?"

Harry thought. Then he said slowly, "It shows us what we want . . . whatever we want . . ."

"Yes and no," said Dumbledore quietly. "It shows us nothing more or less than the deepest, most desperate desire of our hearts . . . However, this mirror will give us neither knowledge or truth. Men have wasted away before it, entranced by what they have seen, or be driven mad, not knowing if what it shows is real or even possible."

That is a frightening notion: a mirror exists which reflects the inward, hidden part of us, the part of us that is our true selves. At any moment, if we were to look in this mirror, we would be faced with the "deepest, most desperate desire of our hearts." That could be an ugly reality to confront. Or it could be a beautiful thing to behold. It could cause us to waste away, driven mad with unfulfilled longing of whether or not what we see could be true. Or it could give us a transformative vision.

Self-Examination, the mirror inside of us, shows us the deepest desire of our hearts. Self-Examination is the practice, in the lovely words of Emily Dickinson, of going out in the darkness with lanterns, looking for ourselves. When we use the mirror of Self-Examination to look inside ourselves, we are finally able to see our real selves.

Self-Examination doesn't give us what we seek; it reveals our souls' longing.

I finally held up the mirror of Self-Examination in a McDonald's in the desert of Arizona after running away from treatment. I was holding a stranger's cell phone, listening to my husband raging, crying out from depths of deep pain. I looked at the mirror inside myself and I saw the deepest desire of my heart: I saw thinness. I saw myself getting dressed and feeling . . . nothing. I had nothing left to fear because I was finally as thin as I ever hoped to be. I saw protruding bones and sunken eyes. I saw pride and control. I saw despair, abuse, and pain. I saw that I was alone. I had chosen the usurper over my husband, my children, my parents, and anyone who had ever cared about me. I saw the end of an ultimatum. I saw I had been seeking nothing . . . nothing.

And that is what I was left with . . . nothing.

I was the prodigal, sent to the fields to feed the pigs.

He [the Prodigal Son] longed to eat his fill from the carob pods the pigs were eating, but no one would give him any. When he *came to his senses,* he said, "How many of my father's hired hands

have more than enough food, and here I am dying of hunger! I'll get up, go to my father, and say to him, Father, I have sinned against heaven and in your sight. I'm no longer worthy to be called your son. Make me like one of your hired hands."
Luke 15:16-19, emphasis added

The Prodigal Son squandered everything his father had given him. He demanded his portion of the inheritance and wasted it. He wasted it and had nothing . . . *nothing* to show for it. But in a moment of Self-Examination, he understood the reality of what he had done. He had sinned against heaven and let immense riches fall through his fingers like water. When all was said and done, he was on the brink of starvation, in a field with pigs. He was worse than the pigs, for they at least had something to eat. As he looked at the mirror inside himself, he *came to his senses*. He had a moment of clarity. Self-Examination did not give him what he needed: food, shelter, reconciliation. It revealed the longing of his heart. It was a personal revelation inspiring him to act.

"So he got up and went to his father. But while the son was still a long way off, his father saw him and was filled with compassion. He ran, threw his arms around his neck, and kissed him" (Luke 15:20). Looking at the mirror inside led the Prodigal Son to grace.

When grace collides with Self-Examination, anything is possible.

In 2010, I returned home from inpatient treatment. The revelation of truth I experienced during my time in the desert had been profound. I had identified the enemy, the usurper, and was ready and willing to fight to overthrow the false king. But being back at home was hard. Everyone—and I mean everyone—now knew what I struggled with. My weight, and its constant fluctuations, seemed to be a matter of public discourse.

The barrage of attention directed at my physical appearance shone a spotlight on my catch-22: I was ashamed of the weight I had been forced to gain while in treatment and longed to lose it. Simultaneously, I was ashamed of how thin I had let myself become and how disgusted others were by my condition. The nature of the comments people made to me constantly reinforced this conundrum.

One Sunday a woman came up to me after church. "My husband said to me that you look like you have the swine flu. I agreed that you look so thin, it seems one good bout of sickness would finish you off. We noticed it today while you were up on the stage playing the piano," she said.

I stood there, reeling in shock at what I had just heard. "But I'm gaining weight," I stammered defensively. "I'm making progress."

"Well, I don't think you should be allowed to be up on the stage in the condition you are in. You are still so thin. What kind of an example is that for our young ladies?"

My body went numb. It was as if she had punched me in the stomach, knocking all the air out of me. *I still looked too thin? I shouldn't be allowed to be on the stage? What more was I supposed to be doing? I really was trying to get better!*

Didn't she know that every inch of progress I had made, every inch of ground I had gained, was covered in my blood and toil? Every fraction of improvement was built at incalculable cost? But what did blood and toil and cost matter to her? They were not her blood and toil and cost—they were mine.

The daily deluge of inspection and evaluation was growing the bitter seed of hopelessness within me, hopelessness that I would never be at peace, never come to terms with gaining weight, never be happy if I could never lose another pound, never be normal and free when it came to eating food, that I would never be an example worthy of emulation. I would always be what I had always been.

No matter how hard I tried.

I felt I was imprisoned in a life over which I had no control, and with each passing day, I began to settle into a cynical agreement of sorts with myself and with God: I would keep on trying to overcome the eating disorder once and for all, I would do my best to disregard what others thought of me, but if I could never actually manage to change, I wouldn't hold it against God. I made a resigned peace with my lot in life. Transformation was an elusive dream . . . for other people. Better people.

As a part of keeping up my end of the bargain with God, I began to attend Celebrate Recovery. Celebrate Recovery is a Christ-centered twelve-step program for anyone with a hurt, habit, or hang-up. Recovery programs are usually associated with drugs and alcohol, but Celebrate Recovery promises a safe place of healing and refuge for anyone: whether the struggle is drugs, alcohol, pornography, codependency, depression, anger, grief, or eating disorders. The idea that I could go somewhere and be myself, free from judging, prying eyes, was very enticing.

I attended meetings, and although I would share when my turn came around the circle, I was careful to play my cards close to the vest. I had spent twenty years living in fear of sharing who I really was with another human being; that habit was not going to break overnight. Honestly, the main reason I attended was that I liked being around people in recovery who had experienced victory. Whether it was over drugs or codependency, their success was a balm to my troubled mind. They were a breath of fresh air in the mire of my church hurt. Their emancipation was a testimony that God was still able to deliver. And if I hung around them long enough, maybe, just maybe . . .

In 2011, I attended the Celebrate Recovery Summit at Saddleback Church. I was excited to go, eager to be a witness to the stories of life change I was sure to hear. The victory others experienced was lovely to behold. They inspired me to believe that change was possible. Of course, according to my wary mind, change was only possible for other people, not me. Recovery was a dream. A beautiful dream.

I sat in the crowd and listened to a woman bravely share her story. She was courage defined, standing there alone, sharing the reality of who she was before thousands of people, galvanized together with expectation and love. I had probably listened to hundreds of testimonies throughout the course of my life, but as I sat there that day, something curious was happening to me. It felt like everything around me was fading; all I could see was the woman on the stage, all I could hear were the words she was speaking. She was speaking directly to me.

She finished sharing and invited her teenage daughter up. The teenage daughter shared and invited her little sister up. The little sister shared and invited her grandmother up. The grandmother shared and invited *her* mother up. Four generations testified. Four generations of proof that freedom was possible. Four generations stood, on the stage, shoulder to shoulder, grinning the toothy, unbridled smile of redemption.

As they stood there, full of joy and freedom, it seemed to me they were standing in a circle of light and sound, and I was at the end of a tunnel looking at them, trying to get to them. But it was if they were far away, in a dream. I felt that if I could get to them, somehow, I could be a part of their beautiful dream. I could have what they had.

How could I get there? How could I possibly have what they had?

I had never wanted anything so much in my whole life. It was the deepest, most desperate desire of my heart. It was a longing for their dream . . . my dream . . . a beautiful, enchanting dream . . . where it didn't matter what I weighed or why I weighed that much;

where I was an example to others, not because of what I looked like, but because I fought the violent fight for my freedom; where my life was the stone of victory cast into the waters, rippling out through the generations.

And then, as is the way with dreams, I was crying, and I didn't know why. Flashes of victory flickered in the circle of light and sound, and I began to sob. Why I had believed that I could never recover? Why had I listened to the words of condemnation: *"What kind of an example do you think you are?"* How could I have never seen that recovery was there all the time?

Once again, I heard the crowd noises, I saw the faces that surrounded me. With a moment of clarity that shook the foundations of my existence, I realized that the women on the stage were not in a dream; they never had been. Recovery was real. It wasn't a dream for other, better people. It was gloriously real.

And it was for me.

In that unguarded moment at the Celebrate Recovery Summit, compelled by the words of truth spoken through the lips of four brave generations, I looked at the mirror inside myself. The mirror made of eternal truth. I saw the deepest longing of my heart; I saw the freedom of the unveiled glory of the Lord reflected there.

Therefore having such a hope, we use great boldness—not like Moses, who used to put a veil over his face so that the sons of Israel could not look at the end of what was fading away. But their minds were closed. For to this day, at the reading of the old covenant, the same veil remains: it is not lifted because it is only set aside in Christ. However, to this day, whenever Moses is read, a veil lies over their hearts, but whenever a person turns to the Lord, the veil is removed. *Now the Lord is the Spirit; and where the Spirit of the Lord is, there is freedom. We all, who with unveiled*

*faces, are reflecting the glory of the Lord and are being transformed
into the same image from glory to; this is from the Lord who is
the Spirit.*
2 Corinthians 3:12-18, emphasis added

As I held up the mirror inside myself at the Celebrate Recovery Summit, grace collided with Self-Examination, and I caught a glimpse of the unveiled glory of the Lord, the ever-increasing glory that called me out of a dream into reality, out of hopelessness into a great and living hope, out of resignation into transformation. All thoughts of bargains with God faded in the light of this revelation. I was beholding something so utterly new and transformative I could not even begin to understand what I would need to do to obtain it. I just knew that I would do anything to get it. It was up to me to embrace the revelation of this new longing: to recover, to once and for all truly recover.

I came home from the Summit and launched myself into the process of Celebrate Recovery. I attended meetings every time the doors were open. This time, when my turn came around the circle to share, I did so with reckless abandon. No matter how worthy or unworthy I felt. No matter how weary I became or how slowly the change was happening. I kept coming back.

I turned my will over to my one and only true Higher Power on a daily basis. I faced my demons by taking a searching and fearless inventory of my life. I found a sponsor and shared my deepest hurts and darkest secrets with her. I leaned into the idea that recovery is a decision followed by a process. I completed a twelve-step study, working the life-giving steps. I had mucked about with them before, but this time, I meant business. Freedom was going to be mine.

I would not take no for an answer.

There were moments when I began to doubt. People hurt me,

and I craved to return to my old ways. But always I remembered those women on the stage. I remembered their redemption smiles and how much I wanted what they had. Self-Examination gave me a longing for the freedom of the unveiled Christ. For you see, longing in the nail-scarred hands of the Savior will always draw us back to the place we were meant to be. It is a place of irresistible transformation.

Longing drew me there that day at the Summit. It draws me there still.

Self-Examination is a practice. It is the practice of facing the deepest, most desperate desire of our hearts with brutal honesty and allowing what we see to inspire us to action. There are two mirrors: You can waste away before the outer mirror, or allow yourself to be transformed by the inner mirror.

CHAPTER 13

Unspeakable

Heaven knows we need never be ashamed of our tears,
for they are rain upon the blinding dust of earth, overlying
our hard hearts. I was better after I had cried than before—
more sorry, more aware of my own ingratitude, more gentle.

"GREAT EXPECTATIONS," CHARLES DICKENS

Carry one another's burdens;
in this way you will fulfill the law of Christ.

GALATIANS 6:2

QUESTION 4: What Am I Doing With Feelings
That Are Too Much to Bear?

HALEY

I was about fourteen or fifteen. It was my freshmen to sophomore year of high school. I had to weigh in, in gym class, and my gym teacher told me I was obese. . . . After he told me, I asked to go to the bathroom and I cried in the locker room alone. I started skipping meals a lot. At least two a day. I would make excuses to miss dinner at home . . . I would stand in front of the mirror and cry, I would pinch my stomach and punch it and tell myself how ugly it was. I would tell myself I hated myself and I did. I absolutely hated myself at that point . . .

JILL

I have been in recovery for bulimia. It started in my late twenties, but I have had issues with food from way before. I'm also in recovery for childhood sexual abuse, physical abuse, domestic violence, and rape. . . . So I just have too much going on. I'm not healed yet and battle with it every day. I hate my body and the way I look. I know Jesus will heal me but I don't feel that He is working on me yet. I'm not strong and trying to focus on small steps. . . . And diets don't work. I've tried them all.

TRACY

My issue started when I was a very young girl. I grew to hate my body because the man who raised me forced me to give my body away to other men that he would trade me off to or even sell. I would do all I could to hide under oversize clothes, because even at the young age of eight I was told I had a body grown women would dream of having. I was so ashamed of having something that made them want to touch me in the ways that they did. As I grew older, I realized that the man who raised me didn't like larger bodies on women, so I started eating as much as I could. . . . I put on quite a bit of weight in three short months. . . . I finally stood up to his advances. . . . It was so easy putting on the weight, but now I cannot get it off no matter how hard I try to this very day. . . . I am a stress eater and have to force myself to stop eating when my stress level is maxed out. I need to get with the program, because the weight I gained this year could potentially take my life. . . .

LISA

I developed at a very early age. I was always slender and this unwanted development drew negative attention from much older men. I remember specifically walking home from the bus stop in sixth grade and getting catcalled by an older married man who had started sitting on his front porch to watch me walk home. At this point in my life I was already in a C cup and I learned that my body was not safe and it betrayed me. I battled throughout middle school with food, trying to morph my body into something that was socially acceptable. I thought that if I could just eat as little as possible, I could lose enough weight to make my breasts go away. This would be followed by a vicious cycle of binge eating and vomiting and ultimately hospitalization. By nineteen, I was married, in an abusive relationship and expecting a child. I ate whatever I wanted and my weight ballooned. . . . My much older husband was a fitness trainer and an extremist about calorie intake, etc. The more abusive the relationship became, the more I ate because it disgusted him. I learned that if I could morph my body into something big, then I would be left alone.

TARA

I was ten in fourth grade. The belt I was wearing was fastened on the loosest hole. I felt insecure and self-conscious and panicked because it wasn't on the tightest. I felt paranoid. I felt that everyone was watching me, judging me, and I thought it was because I was too big. I thought I had to be smaller, shorter, and petite to be feminine. That belt was evidence that I wasn't. I felt ashamed. I tightened my belt as far as it would go until it broke. Now I was even more ashamed and embarrassed.

VANESSA

I've disliked my body for as long as I can remember . . . but I don't know why. . . . I was a people pleaser and I grew up in performance-based environment. . . . My first husband, who was abusive, told me I was fat. . . . My goal was to make him happy. That's when

I started using food in a disordered way (though not by choice). . . .
He would have me up at midnight cooking huge meals and expecting me to eat with him. Then during the day I would try to diet.
Once I got away from him, went to college, and got a good paying job, I realized I could buy myself all the food items I had ever
longed for. So unhealthy eating and yo-yo diets continued from
there. . . . Little by little I am learning to eat healthy and to focus
on that instead of dieting and the way that I look, but it is so very
difficult.

BRENDA

I was very overweight by age nine, using food to cope in an alco-
holic home. I was called names at elementary school, started hating
my body, and as a result began forty years of dieting, weight loss/
gain, and body image issues. Exacerbated by a few years of getting
lots of "positive" attention for my body when I was "thin" at times
during junior high and high school.

CARISSA

I was nine and had to wear a bra because I was overweight and
not because I was busty. At a young age, while I was going through
sexual abuse, my stepfather would load my plate, then force me to
eat until I threw up; then he would make me continue eating. You
would think I would hate food, but that is my struggle.

I don't know what emotions you go through reading these
stories, but as my mind plays the picture of the hell these women
have gone through, I feel myself drowning. I can't breathe with the
sorrow and pain just imagining these moments of trauma. It's too
much to bear just to think of it. But to actually experience these
excruciating, terrifying, shame-filled, heart-shredding moments . . .

WHAT DO YOU DO WITH FEELINGS THAT ARE TOO MUCH TO BEAR?

I recently scrolled through Facebook and came across a Timehop post from three years ago, written by a sweet friend. She wrote, in part, "Thank God the past is the past, but sometimes it is a blessing to mentally retrace where you have been. In doing so you are reminded of what you lost in the process and what has been gained through His healing."

I liked the old post and browsed the comment section to read the past and present responses and leave a grateful comment of my own. A beautiful young face stopped me cold. It was the profile picture of one who had responded to the post those many years ago. It was as if she were looking at me, her gaze turning upward to the camera, lovely features frozen in time.

Tears streamed down my cheeks as I read the questions she asked:

What if . . . you still feel alone or more isolated and the more you seek Jesus, the more you feel pain? What if you don't feel love . . . you were just forgotten? What if the more you praise, the more unnoticed you become?

She never received satisfactory answers to those raw, searching questions. She has since been found dead in her home, a victim of her addiction.

"What if . . . . the more you seek Jesus, the more you feel pain?"
What do you do with feelings that are too much to bear?

One summer, when I was about three years into my recovery, I sat in a church service full of teenagers. The evangelist onstage performed an array of histrionics as he paced back and forth, recounting a time he had attended a ministers' conference. "At one point they broke us up into small groups. They gave each of us a piece of paper and asked us to write, as honestly as possible, the one thing we wished our parents had done for us." He paused for dramatic effect. "I mean, I wrote that I wished my parents had taken me to McDonald's more. But there were grown men, lots of them, and they were crying. They were crying about their parents getting a divorce when they were children!" His face was incredulous with disbelief, "I think it's safe to say if you are a fully grown man still crying about something that happened when you were a kid, it's high time you got over it!"

There have been a few moments in my life when the Scripture came alive to me. This was one of those moments. I could feel, with utmost clarity and complete understanding, what Jesus was feeling when He took out His whip and started overturning tables at the Temple.

How dare he.

How dare he stand in derision over those who had experienced pain he could never begin to fathom? The room was filled with teenagers. Turning to my left and to my right, I saw a sea of young faces, looking up, their expressions fervent. They had come as pilgrims, looking to this evangelist for an answer.

What do you do with feelings that are too much to bear?

There was a girl, told she was obese in front of the class, forced to find shelter in the locker room. She sobbed, her heart crushed with humiliation.

"You are obese. You are wrong," she told herself.

What does she do with feelings that are too much to bear?

There was a little girl, abused by someone who should have protected her. She had been used, hope slowly slipping away from her.

"My body betrayed me. This is my fault," she told herself.

What does she do with feelings that are too much to bear?

There was a woman, closer to the middle of life than the beginning. She looked in a mirror and listened to the sound of silence.

"You are disgusting. He is never coming back, and you are to blame," she told herself.

What does she do with feelings that are too much to bear?

There was a woman mourning the untimely death of her grown son. In the face of devastating tragedy, she coped with life the only way she knew how. She binged and purged and binged and purged, trying to fill spaces that would never be filled again.

"You are worthless. Your reason for living is gone," she told herself.

What does she do with feelings that are too much to bear?

To the question "What do you do with feelings that are too much to bear?" the usurper, the desires that war against your spirit, would say, "Those feelings really are too much to bear. One person couldn't possibly handle feeling all of those feelings. You need me. I have an enticing solution. I can offer you all the control you have ever dreamed of. Come let us reason together . . . you need to feel numb. You need to feel . . . nothing. Feeling nothing is safe . . . push feeling deep inside . . . bury it with the past. Bury it with yourself."

The usurper knows that when your emotions are consigned to the grave, hidden within dark corners of the tomb inside you, it will finally be free to take what it does not have the right to take. It will take *you*.

The usurper, your flesh, wants to be god. Never forget that. The usurper is ever seeking to convince you to find fulfillment apart from the love, grace, and mercy of Christ.

The usurper says, "If you open yourself up to emotions, you will just get hurt."

The usurper says, "Expect nothing from anyone; that way you will never be disappointed."

The usurper says, "Your body betrayed you. It needs to suffer. It needs to go away."

The usurper says, "A loving God would never allow someone to experience so much pain."

The usurper says, "Once you start crying, you will never stop."

The usurper says, "The story of your life will end with a lonely gravestone, the only proof you ever existed."

The usurper wants to be god. It wants to set itself up as a high king and dictator over you. It wants you to view "feelings that are too much to bear" as dirty, useless things that need to be thrown away. But make no mistake—the usurper is *not* God. The real, living, one true God does not view "feelings that are too much to bear" as shameful, disposable trash. He sees them as incalculably valuable, because Jesus Christ Himself went to great lengths to redeem them.

> He was despised and rejected by men,
>   a man of suffering.
> Like one from whom people hide their faces
>   he was despised, and we held him in low esteem.
> Surely he took up our pain and bore our suffering . . .
> Isaiah 53:3-4, niv

The one true and living King knows what suffering feels like. He knows betrayal and heartache. He is acquainted with rejection. All of the emotions that suffocate our spirits with immovable weight, Jesus experienced and took upon Himself. From the manger to His mother's arms, from the Temple to the wilderness, from the Sea of Galilee to the Last Supper, from the cross to the tomb, the empty tomb, He took them.

Surely He bore our sorrows.

Therefore, since we have a great high priest who has passed through the heavens—Jesus the Son of God—let us hold fast to the confession. For we do not have a high priest who is unable to sympathize with our weaknesses, but One who has been tested in every way as we are, yet without sin. Therefore let us then approach the throne of grace with boldness, so that we may receive mercy and find grace to help us at the proper time .
Hebrews 4:14-16

Jesus understands what it feels like to feel. Jesus, the great High Priest, has faced the question "What do I do with feelings that are too much to bear?"

Then Jesus came with them to a place called Gethsemene, and He told the disciples, "Sit here while I go over there and pray." Taking along Peter and two sons of Zebedee, He began to be sorrowful and deeply distressed. Then He said to them, "My soul is swallowed up in sorrow—to the point of death. Remain here and stay awake with Me." Going a little farther, He fell facedown and prayed, "My Father! If it is possible, let this cup pass from Me. Yet not as I will, but as you will."
Matthew 26:36-39

Jesus was sorrowful to the point of death. Have you ever felt so sad you thought you were going to die? The thought of what was to come was unfathomable. Yet, in the face of such unbearable knowledge, Jesus made a choice: He chose to admit that He was "overwhelmed with sorrow to the point of death." He decided to let Himself be vulnerable, to tell His Father how He felt, how He really felt . . . and to trust Him with those feelings. "My Father, if it is possible, may this cup be taken from me. Yet not as I will, but as you will."

Being vulnerable may seem like the last thing you should do in the face of overwhelming emotions. It is contrary to what you have always believed. God helps those who help themselves, right? How could you possibly entertain letting another person know who you really are? Some of your emotions were borne of experiences that were not your fault, but some were borne of the shameful things you have done. Why would you willingly and recklessly offer up the most fragile, painful part of who you are? It makes no sense. How could there possibly be any value in doing so? What kind of freedom could ever be attained from something so ridiculous, so terrifying?

Vulnerability is simply sharing who you are, with no holds barred. It is the act of standing upon the truth and allowing the truth to set you free. Brené Brown wrote, "Shame derives its power from being unspeakable." It is attracted to darkness and unspoken pain; it needs those things to take root and grow. When you confess your faults, your secrets, your failures, and your sin to another human being, you rip shame out and discard it like the useless weed that it is.

At this point you may be asking, "So you are telling me that the answer to the question 'What do I do with feelings that are too much to bear?' is to share *who I am* with another human being? Another human being who might laugh at me, judge me, and ridicule me? Another human being who might possibly take the shattered pieces I give them and throw them back in my face?"

The life-changing power of vulnerability has nothing to do with the amount of empathy the other person possesses or even what they do with what you give them. It has everything to do with *you being vulnerable*. The power is in the process; *the process changes you.*

Vulnerability is found in different places for different people. I found it in a church recovery group, a Christ-centered twelve-step program called Celebrate Recovery. For me, the church had always been a place where failing was not allowed. Or at least, if you did fail, you should have the decency to never speak of it; being down on your luck was considered a symptom of the systemic dysfunction of your faith. It was hard for me to fathom that a place like Celebrate Recovery existed. Celebrate Recovery was a place that took the words of Scripture seriously— *"Confess your sins to one another and pray for one another"*; a place to be fully transparent and honest, embracing the lovely and unlovely, triumph and tragedy, as things to be experienced in community with others, to offer to God, to be redeemed by God; to put our hope and value and identity not in the transformation we are seeking, but in the Transformer.

I first learned of Celebrate Recovery through my husband. He had fully embraced the recovery process for himself, working on his own issues with codependency. As I observed the positive changes in him, I became intrigued. Could it really be true? Was there really a place, in a church no less, where people said what they struggled with—*out loud*—in front of other people? That kind of foolhardiness seemed diametrically opposed to what I had always believed: strong people had hard times, but they pulled themselves up by their bootstraps. And yet . . . I could see that my husband had allowed himself to be vulnerable at Celebrate Recovery and was changing right before my eyes. I wanted what he had.

I wanted the power of God that is perfected in weakness.

Before Celebrate Recovery, I was afraid of vulnerability. I wasn't necessarily worried about what others would think of me, although that was a small part of it. I was convinced beyond any doubt that voicing actual words gave them power over my life. As long as the insidious lie, misguided belief, or deep fear remained concealed in the darkness of my own soul, it was held in check and was protected from being allowed to reach its destructive potential. Confession was tantamount to invitation—if I spoke it out loud, then it was destined to come to pass. If I were to share, *out loud,* the greatest fear in my heart, that I was afraid my daughters would develop eating disorders as a result of my poor example, then guess what would happen? *BAM!* The other cosmic shoe would surely drop.

I had always been admonished, "You better watch what you are inviting to happen. I know you think you need peace right now, but if you go around saying out loud that you want God to send you peace, well, guess what? He is going to send the mother of all trials into your life to show you what peace really means!" Or, "I know you think you need to share the feelings of pain and regret you are experiencing because you lived a promiscuous life, but *watch out!* The old lascivious desires will come back big-time if you start talking about them. I mean, the devil can hear what you are saying!"

These alarmist words drove me to a place of fear; I was convinced that somehow I possessed the ability to conjure calamity out of thin air by the power of my words alone. Or worse, fear that God wasn't sovereign and loving after all . . . that He viewed vulnerability as a defect of character too great for His grace to overcome. He was capricious and changeable, so I had better *watch out!*

The truth is, fearful beliefs such as these are diametrically opposed to who God really is. They are motivated by a theology that places me in control of God. These beliefs are a form of superstition that make vulnerability seem like a monster under the bed, patiently lying in wait to attack and devour. They distort vulnerability's real beauty.

Vulnerability was God's idea in the first place.

Christ Jesus, who, existing in the form of God,
did not consider equality with God

as something to be used for His own advantage.
Instead He emptied Himself
by assuming the form of a slave,
taking on the likeness of men.
And when He had come as a man
in His external form,
He humbled Himself by becoming obedient
to the point of death—
even to death on a cross.
Philippians 2:5-8

The incarnation of Christ was God's greatest act of love and vulnerability.

You cannot experience being truly loved by God until you have experienced vulnerability. When you allow yourself to become vulnerable and transparent, voicing the deepest part of who you are—your abuses, hopes, dreams, fears, doubts, failures, and successes—to another human being, you are really offering up yourself to God. To be fully known and fully loved.

Timothy Keller wrote:

To be loved but not known is comforting but superficial. To be known and not loved is our greatest fear. But to be fully known and truly loved is, well, a lot like being loved by God. It is what we need more than anything. It liberates us from pretense, humbles us out of our self-righteousness, and fortifies us for any difficulty life can throw at us.

God isn't waiting in the heavens to pounce on the pitiful words you say, opening the floodgates of misfortune. He is waiting, waiting like the father waited for the prodigal, to embrace the words you tentatively offer, wrapping them up in His love, overwhelming them with His grace.

But wait—there's more!

Something else happens when you open up your heart to another human being. Not only are you able to experience being both fully known and fully loved by God, you are able to cultivate a life-changing common bond with that other person. It is the kind of bond that exists when someone listens to the words you say and responds, "I know exactly what you mean. I have done the same thing. I have felt the same way." Better still, if that common bond of vulnerability is shared with another believer, you are then able to hold each other up and encourage each other in prayer.

I found this to be more than true, especially in Celebrate Recovery step studies. I developed friendships there that will last my whole life long. When I grow tired and prone to discouragement, they lift me up and challenge me to keep on fighting the good fight.

Two are better than one
  because they have a good reward for their efforts.
For if either falls,
  his companion can lift him up."
Ecclesiastes 4:9, niv

THE GREAT WALL

Once I began the process of experiencing true vulnerability, there was no turning back. I was hooked—on the new relationships I found, the new freedom to be myself, the new victories I was winning over the usurper as I systematically dismantled its labyrinth of lies and shame. I was standing amazed day by day, at the love, mercy, and grace of God, who was proving "There is no fear in love; instead, perfect love drives out fear…" (1 John 4:18, niv).

However, even amid my positive transformation, people still found a way to criticize me. They presented this criticism as *concern* for my spiritual welfare. "Why do you need to keep bringing up the past? It's the *past*. Your wounds will never heal if you keep picking at them. Why do you need to keep picking at something that should be behind you?" Or, "Why do you need to keep talking about all of the destruction and devastation that happened to you? There is nothing you can do about it now. You can't change what happened, so why keep reminding yourself? Why remember?"

Why remember?

Why remember destruction and devastation? Why remember suffering and abuse? Why remember sin and shame? Why remember the sound of the door as it closed behind the person that brought those things to you? Why remember being alone, behind that closed door, staring at the peeling paint on the ceiling, wondering how you could ever feel happy again? Why remember all of the things you wish you could undo? Why remind yourself what is so painful to remember?

It seemed absurd to the people who demanded an answer to the question "Why remember?" It was counterintuitive to them that one would look back with the express intention of confronting pain. They spent their lives constructing a spiritual reality they were comfortable understanding. Being vulnerable was messy . . . it was full of unknowns . . . it could get out of hand quickly . . . it could cause them to have to look at human suffering. And then what?

I would answer that question, "Why remember?" with two responses.

First, **we remember because it mattered to you and it certainly mattered to God.** David wrote in Psalm 56:8, "You Yourself [God] have recorded my wanderings. Put my tears in Your bottle. Are they not in your records?"

It mattered when you cried yourself to sleep in the loneliness of the night. Your suffering was not meaningless. It shaped who you would become and influenced every decision you made. It formed the fabric of your life. It was not insignificant that you struggled to find purpose, wrestled with doubt, tried and failed and tried and failed and tried and failed. Every second of every minute of every joy and every pain is you. And you matter. Therefore, what you felt and what you experienced have significance. The Bible itself is the greatest example of remembering. It is full of countless stories of mankind, his frailty and his triumph. The Bible, and all of its remembering, accomplishes the same thing our remembering does: it is the living proof that we matter to God and Jesus came to make all things new.

Second, I would answer the question "Why remember?" with another question. **How can you rebuild a wall if you never examine the ruins to see why it fell down in the first place?**

Nehemiah wrote:

After I arrived in Jerusalem and had been there three days, I got up at night and took a few men with me . . . I went out at night through the Valley Gate toward the Serpent's Well and the Dung Gate, and I inspected the walls of Jerusalem that had been broken down and its gates that had been destroyed by fire. . . . The officials did not know where I had gone or what I was doing, for I had not yet told the Jews, priest, nobles, officials, or the rest of those who would be doing the work. So I said to them, "You see the trouble we are in. Jerusalem lies in ruins and its gates have been burned down. Come, let's rebuild Jerusalem's wall, so that we will no longer be a disgrace."
Nehemiah 2:11-13, 16-17

Nehemiah possessed the vision and the passion to begin the process of rebuilding Jerusalem's wall, which had been in ruins for over a hundred years since its destruction by the Babylonians. There is much that could be shared about the life of Nehemiah—he played a significant role in the restoration of Jerusalem and was a man of great influence. Amid the details of his remarkable life, there is one thing worthy of notice that would be easy to disregard. He "inspected the walls of Jerusalem that had been broken down and its gates that had been destroyed by fire."

It was a profoundly simple thing to do. Inspect the damage. Assess what had been destroyed and what needed repaired. Looking, with his own eyes, at the extent of the destruction. He could have never formed a reconstruction plan if he had not done this first, simple thing.

Remembering enables you to survey the damage that has been done to you, to your wall. It doesn't matter if the destruction was perpetrated by someone else or by you. The structure of your wall has been compromised, and you need to restore it. Unless you see, with your own eyes, the places that have been broken down, it is impossible to begin to rebuild correctly. Until you do this, you will just be piling bricks up indiscriminately, heaping them on places that are still standing, fortifying the wrong areas, making the wall just as compromised as it was before. The broken-down and burned-out sections of the wall need restoration, not the ones that remain standing.

There is no shame is looking at the physical ruins of an actual wall that has been damaged to ascertain what needs to be done to make it whole again. Likewise, there is no shame in remembering what you have done and what has been done to you in order to restore the places within you that have been broken down and burned out. Remembering allows you to do just that.

William Shakespeare wrote in *Macbeth,* "Give sorrow words: the grief that does not speak whispers the o'er-fraught heart and bids it break."

"Give sorrow words . . ." Sometimes it isn't pretty; it can be repulsive. It can be terrifying, and it is most likely the last thing you ever

imagined you would have the strength to do. But once you give yourself permission to feel and express sorrow, joy, confusion, depression, embarrassment, rejection, pride, humiliation, happiness, pain, loneliness, and all the emotions you have been desperately trying to make go away through your eating disorder and other destructive behaviors, shame begins to lessen its grip. The power of silent guilt and invisible pain begin to crumble.

The unspeakable has found a voice.

CHAPTER 14

Twinkling of an Eye

Death be not proud, though some have called thee
Mighty and dreadfull, for, thou art not soe,
For, those, whom thou think'st, thou dost overthrow,
Die not, poor death, nor yet canst thou kill mee.

SONNET X, JOHN DONNE

QUESTION 5: Am I Pursuing a Perfect Body or a Perfected Body?

A TALE OF TWO LAND ROVERS

Imagine that two different people purchased identical Land Rovers. Brand-new off the lot—all the bells and whistles and upgrades possible, shiny paint and new car smell, every bit a luxury car. And every bit an extremely capable four-wheel drive, off-road vehicle.

One person drove their Land Rover to a lovely, suburban home, taking an extra lap or two around the block for the sake of the neighbors' prying eyes. (Selfie in front of the car!) Housed safely in the attached garage, great care was taken to protect it from the elements. It was a pride and joy to drive to school, to work, and to the soccer field. Any mud that found its way onto the gleaming outer surface was removed immediately. There was no sign of rust because it was meticulously washed every weekend, displayed in the driveway in full magnificent splendor. In this manner, this Land Rover spent its days, protected and fanatically cared for, taking the safe and familiar roads, never venturing off the beaten path.

The other person drove their Land Rover to the Mexican border. After crossing, they continued a thousands-of-miles journey into Central America, finally arriving in El Salvador. The capital, San Salvador, is a bustling city, teeming with life. The phrase "may the best man win" aptly describes the experience of driving there; every maneuver requires daring, nerve, and a certain disregard for the rules of the road. From there, the Land Rover ventured to the outer reaches of civilization. Winding its way clinging to the side of a mountain, splashing through rivers of muddy water, traversing roads with more potholes than asphalt, this Land Rover was used hard. It carried medical supplies, food, clothing, agricultural equipment, shovels for well digging, and Bibles. It was put to hard use by the missionary who purchased it from the car lot on that day many years ago, when it was gleaming and unspoiled.

After ten years, these two Land Rovers look very different. They both have been taken care of; for all the wear and tear the missionary put on his Land Rover, he never did anything unnecessarily reckless. When the oil needed changing, he changed it. He cleaned it, when time allowed. He never drove it off the side of a cliff for the sheer fun of it. But time and the rigors of life on the mission field produced more than a few dents and scratches on its once-pristine exterior. The other Land Rover, however, is looking very well preserved—low mileage, not a scratch or dent to be found. Even the tires appear to have every groove on the tread intact. It is every bit the grand specimen it had been on the day of its purchase.

In this tale of two Land Rovers, which vehicle had more worth? Which vehicle possessed more value? I suppose it would depend on the standard by which value is judged. A case could be made that the near-mint Land Rover was more valuable by virtue of its condition. Its blue book value would be considered "excellent," and as such, it would be worth more money. But the missionary's Land Rover . . . by what standard could its worth be determined? More than a little worn down and more than a little unsightly, it was a luxury vehicle well squandered on the less-traveled roads. Roads that led to communities of people long since forgotten by the world, who eked out an existence in the face of daunting circumstances, communities of people who cooked on open fires and toiled to find sanitary drinking water, whose children often died too soon and too often, people with hopes and dreams, with joy and heartache and more than a little sorrow.

How do you feel about your body?

Today. Right now.

That could be a provocative question to ask. Even though you may have embraced eternal perspective and vowed to fight against the usurper, your flesh, with all your might, the fact remains that you still do have a physical body. And that physical body needs contending with. Throughout the course of my four decades on this earth, I have participated in hundreds of therapy groups, open share groups, twelve-step groups, mothers of preschoolers groups, Bible studies, etc. The reason these groups of women assembled varied greatly, and the honesty with which they would share their fears and failures and shortcomings vacillated widely. But there was always one topic that would invariably reduce them to tears, whether they were an addict, a grandmother, a stay-at-home mom, or a teenager: how they felt about themselves and their bodies.

The hatred ran deep.

It had been a long time since the addict heard anyone say anything positive about her or her trashy appearance. Granny definitely looked like she knew her way around the kitchen. Stay-at-home mommy certainly was not beach-body ready. And the teenager had been told by some of her friends that perhaps she should look into bulimia to lose weight faster. So, she did. But she was just as miserable after she tried it as she was before…even more so…the physical pain of purging had taken its toll. She then did something very brave—she reached out and asked for help from the school counselor. Needless to say, word got around that she was a freak when it came to food. As she was walking down the hall one morning, trying to feel invisible, a teenage boy shouted, "Maybe you should give bulimia another try. It looks like you could use it!"

I am the first to recognize there are varying degrees to which women dislike their bodies. I would venture to say that the vast majority of women are dissatisfied with their bodies and appearances, and if they were given the opportunity, would gladly change them. We possess a little ability to modify, disguise, and control what we have inherited, but there is only so much that can actually be done. Our gene pool is what it is, despite our best efforts. This can be, at times, a disheartening and depressing reality to face.

Why is it so devastating to realize that we have such a meager ability to change what we have been given? Who said that our bodies had to be objects of personal scorn? Who are all the people we have set up in our minds as the judges and juries, delivering verdicts on our bodies' worthiness? Why do we believe that the outward physical condition of our bodies has anything to do with real, lasting value? Does God have anything to say about our bodies?

BOUGHT WITH A PRICE

I am 5'9" tall, and for a good, long while throughout my adult life, I weighed less than 100 pounds. I was a walking advertisement for an eating disorder.

I have also weighed more than 100 pounds. Sometimes a good deal more. The times I weighed more than 100 pounds, I also struggled with an eating disorder. The struggle during that period of my life, when I was at a "normal" weight and appearance, was every bit as hellish, maybe more so, than when I looked the part of a woman who obviously degraded her body by unnatural means in order to stay thin.

Appearance is often a poor reflection of what is really going on beneath the surface, in the hidden parts of who we are. There is so much more to us than meets the eye; which is simultaneously terrifying and wondrous. But God, who sees all, the outward and the hidden places, knows all, and loves all. We are fully known. And fully loved.

That is why, to me, one of God's most beautiful characteristics is that He doesn't look at the outward appearance—He looks at the heart. But people…unfortunately, they don't look at the heart so much. They generally only look at the outward appearance.

They look and they judge. Then they become *concerned*.

It was in this way, that I, a pastor's wife, wearing my dysfunction publicly as a garment of shame, received a truckload of godly *concern*. This concern was usually voiced in one familiar, unending refrain. I heard this particular catchphrase of concern so often that, at one point, I considered getting a tattoo across my forehead that said,

"Yes, I am aware that my body is a temple of the Holy Spirit."

That was the endless exhortation. "Don't you know that your body is a temple of the Holy Spirit?"

I was obviously completely unaware that my body was a temple, right? What other explanation could there have possibly been for a woman to so abuse her body? Surely, I must not have known that my body was a temple. Therefore, since I was ignorant of that blessed truth, I needed to be enlightened. Hence, the *concern*.

Really, though, concern had *nothing* to do with making sure I was properly subjugated by the use of weaponized scripture. The spirit in which they communicated the Scripture, "Your body is a temple," was crystal clear. There was a standard and I was missing it. Obviously.

One day, when I was obviously struggling, an elder's wife invited me out to lunch. I was flattered that someone so esteemed in the church wanted to spend time with me. As the meal commenced and the conversation began to flow, this woman, who had so graciously asked me to lunch, made this pronouncement, "God wants you to know that your body is a temple and He is not pleased with the way you have been treating it."

The food I had just taken a bite of turned to sawdust in my mouth. I began to stammer, crumbs cascading from my lips, "I know...I'm trying...I'll do better. I promise," I scrambled for the right way to express that I accepted my deserved chastisement. It was an incontrovertible fact, after all.

My body was a temple and God was not pleased with me. Not at all.

*Your body is a temple...how dare you so insolently lay waste to the majesty of the temple of God...how dare you deliberately vandalize the dwelling place of the Most High...*These thoughts constantly rattled around in the recesses of my mind. Every time I skipped a meal, every time I succumbed to a sugary craving, every time I purged, the death-rattle grew louder...YOUR BODY IS A TEMPLE. FOR THE SAKE OF ALL THAT IS GOOD AND HOLY, TRY HARDER!

It was a bitter pill to swallow; but swallow it I must. It was the medicine that promised freedom and Godliness. How could I ever have credibility as a representative of Christ if my temple looked like a hot mess? I needed to treat my body better if I wished to be certified as a suitable temple in which the Holy Spirit of the God could reside. That was the ticket to pleasing God.

I've painted a picture of the ways the Scripture, "Your body is a temple," was thrown at me in hand grenade fashion, by others and by myself. We tend to assign judgment when we wield the statement, "your body is a temple."

Your body is a temple... *You chain-smoking, tattooed, sugar-indulging, temple-defiler. Stop smoking, repent of the body art, stop eating sugar (and for the love of God, EXERCISE), and maybe then, your temple will be worthy for God to call it His home.*

Perhaps at this point you may be thinking, *well, it's unfortunate that you had a negative experience with the way that Scripture was used, but it doesn't negate the fact that it is true. Our bodies are the temples of the Holy Spirit. We owe it to God to keep them healthy.*

For the sake of being agreeable, let's say that we agree. (Although, if we apply proper exegesis to the Scriptures in 1 Corinthians that refer to the body as a temple, we would find that they have nothing to do with the condition of the physical body as related to health, exercise, diet, and physical appearance.) (But, I digress.)

If we agree that our bodies deserve to be kept healthy, who then defines what "keeping our bodies healthy" looks like? Who then defines what "keeping our bodies healthy" even *is*? Are you prepared to be the judge of that? Are you prepared to be the judge of who is or is not a temple defiler? If someone is confined to a wheelchair, does it matter if the tragedy that put them there was the result of their own recklessness or the result of someone else's? Or was it God's fault? Should it matter? The end result is the same: a broken down temple. Would you judge someone with type 2 diabetes as a temple defiler? Someone who goes to Weight Watchers? Someone who has anorexia? Someone who has cancer? Are they a temple defiler? Their temples have been defiled, there is no denying that.

You might say, "The person with type 2 diabetes caused her condition, but person with cancer did not." Are you sure about that? What kind of cancer did she have? Did she eat too much soy? How about heart disease? Was it stress-induced? Hereditary? Did her father have heart disease, too?

Are blame and intent considerations when we deem a body a worthy temple or not? Who then judges *that?* Who then judges the intentions of a person's heart? You? Or me?

It is said the road to hell is paved with good intentions; or at the very least, it is paved with the judgments of what others believe our intentions ought to be. Which is sad. It is a tragedy that the things we all have in common with one another—our humanity and our deep-rooted need to find meaning in this life—are dissected and judged and found wanting.

It's equally a tragedy that the very language, "Your body is a temple of the Holy Spirit," has been hijacked to mean something diametrically opposed to its original intent. *And the original intent was beautifully revolutionary.*

When the Apostle Paul wrote the words "Your body is a temple" to the church in Corinth, he was saying this: You no longer have to go to an ornate, gilded temple, built with your blood, toil and sacrifice in order to meet with your god. No, now *you* are the temple. *You* are the place in which your God will dwell. And your God has built this temple in you with His own blood, toil and sacrifice.

How typical of human nature to take this radical, free gift of love and immediately turn it back into what it was before. Only now, instead of requiring a suitable building, we demand a suitable physical body; maintained in accordance with strict rules and regulations, in the great hope that it will be considered good enough for a holy God to make His habitation there.

Make no mistake, the holy God that humbled Himself to death, even death on a Cross, does not require a temple adorned with perfect ornamentation, in keeping with the fashions of the day.

He requires one thing: a yielded heart.

Looking back at that pastor's wife in the restaurant, who was me, shamed and defeated, I often feel sad. I wish I could talk to her. I wish I could slip into the seat beside her and squeeze her hand and assure her that God's feelings for her had nothing to do with the way she was treating her body. But I know that I can't. And I know that I wouldn't, even if I could. That shame choked moment was refining me, even then. A seed of defiance had been planted; the kind of defiance that looks lies and injustice in the face and declares, "No more!" Or in my case, to declare, "This way of thinking and speaking to others is not helpful at all. Using Scripture in this way is at best, irresponsible, and at worst, damning."

For the Word of God is not a message of condemnation. It is good news of great joy for all people.

> Do you not know that your body is a temple of the Holy Spirit who is in you, whom you have from God, and that you are not your own? For *you have been bought with a price:* therefore glorify God in your body.
> 1 Corinthians 6:19-20, nasb, emphasis added

As a believer in Christ, the temple of my body already *is* worthy for God to call it His home. It became worthy the minute Jesus suffered and died, giving His life as a ransom for many. The minute the angels clothed in robes of white lightning, sentinels to an empty tomb, said, "Why are you looking for the living among the dead? He is not here, but He has been resurrected!" (Luke 24:5).

Yes, there is a standard. But, yes! God already met that standard. We have been bought with a price. *Therefore,* we honor God with our bodies. Not the other way around. "In view of God's mercies… offer your bodies as a living sacrifice, holy and pleasing to God" (Romans 12:1, niv). We don't offer our bodies to obtain mercy. We offer them because His mercy has already been given. The writers of the New Testament vehemently fought against the legalism of the pharisees, to the point of laying down their very lives, to make sure this beautiful, revolutionary order of operations was kept straight: We honor God because He *first* loved us.

How wonderfully liberating this realization is. This realization turns condemnation on its head. It strips the world's standards—what we are conditioned to believe our physical bodies are supposed to be—of all power to define who we are in Christ. I don't need a fit temple. I need a temple that is filled with the resurrected glory of the Holy Spirit. And guess what? I already have that! I don't need to restore my temple. My temple was restored the moment "God loved the world in this way: He gave His One and Only Son, so that everyone who believes in Him will not perish, but have eternal life." (John 3:16)

I am a suitable temple because I have been bought with a price.

The usurper subverts the truth, "You have been bought with a price," to strategically deceive us. The flesh wants to be god, after all. It will do anything to give itself the upper hand. The enemy says, "Your body is yours. It is your responsibility to glorify God by treating your body the right way—how else could it ever be good enough for God? This is how you prove you are a legitimate temple in which God can reside."

If you are a believer in Christ, the eternal is now. You have been bought with a great price. That changes everything. "God raised up the Lord and will also raise us up by His power" (1 Corinthians 6:14). Your body does not exist for you to mold and make it into what you feel is most pleasing to you. It exists for you to offer to God, to be used by God, and to be redeemed by God. You are forever being drawn back to the reality that you are created in God's image, therefore you have value to God. You have been bought with a price.

And it was a great price, indeed.

MY BODY, A VEHICLE

What would happen if we began viewing our physical bodies in a new way? What would happen if we began to believe that our bodies are invaluable vehicles to be offered to the Creator as living sacrifices instead of well-preserved cultural showpieces to protect and perfect? What if they traversed the narrow ways? What if we viewed them in light of what they have done, and for whom they have done it, instead of how meticulously maintained they look? What if we measured their value in their ability to get us where we needed to go? (And where are we going, indeed?) What if our bodies were vehicles? What if our bodies were vehicles created in the image of God?

Ravi Zacharias said this:

The first thing I want to remind you of is this, is that we are told according to the Scriptures, prior to the resurrection story, that God is the author of human essence. God is the author, in the essential nature of our humanity. We didn't come into being by accident. We just didn't suddenly appear unconceived or without any purpose in mind, but that God Himself is the designer and brought us into existence. The psalmist says, "When I see the heavens, the work of your hands, the sun and moon and the stars which you have made. What is there in man that you are mindful of him?" (Psalm 8:3-4). This fact of our creation is a vital source in enabling us to understand what it means to be human. It's a vital source, giving us the generality of our essence, created in the image of God. Some of you have probably heard me [Ravi Zacarais] mention the simple conversation between Jesus and the one who was questioning Him, trying to pit Him against Caesar. And he looked at Jesus and he said, "Is it all right to pay taxes to Caesar?" . . . Jesus, so brilliant in His response, He says, "Give me a coin." And He took the coin and He says, "Whose image do you see on this?" The man says, "Caesar's." Jesus says, "Give to Caesar that which is Caesar's, and give to God that which is God's" (Mark 12:14-17). The disingenuousness of the questioner is noticed in the fact that he did not come back with a second question. He should have said, "What belongs to God?" And Jesus would have said, "Whose image is on you?"

The idea that our bodies are vehicles may seem too mundane and too practical to provide inspiration. But the idea that our bodies are vehicles is anything but mundane because of this beautiful truth: our bodies have been made in the image of God. From the moment God breathed the breath of life into His human creation way back in the Garden of Eden when He said, "Let Us make man in Our own image," He was telling us something about Himself. The very fact we have bodies created in God's likeness means that *He designed us with a purpose in mind.* He wanted us to be able to know Him. One of the ways we can know Him is by the form and function of the physical bodies He fashioned from the dust of the earth. Believing that our bodies are vehicles sets us free from the tyranny of feeling we are responsible for making our bodies worthy of use. God created them in His image. They already are worthy of use. They are worthy vehicles to do the work of the eternal Kingdom; whether in glory or suffering, whether in accomplishment or failure, whether in thinness or not-so-thinness, whether in youthfulness or old age, whether in sickness or health, whether in life or death, they are worthy.

My body is a vehicle, made in the image of God, bought with a great price. **Therefore my goal in life, in regard to my physical body, is this: A perfected body, not a perfect one.** I will not spend my days and my effort and my precious time in pursuit of a perfect body. I will pursue a perfected body.

Now if Christ is preached as raised from the dead, how can some of you say, "There is no resurrection of the dead"? But if there is no resurrection of the dead, then Christ has not been raised; and if Christ has not been raised, then our preaching is without foundation, and so is your faith. . . .

But now Christ has been raised from the dead . . .

But someone will say, "How are the dead raised? What kind of a body will they have when they come?" Foolish one! What you sow does not come to life unless it dies. And as for what you sow—you are not sowing the future body, but only a seed. . . .

Sown in corruption, raised in incorruption;
sown in dishonor, raised in glory;
sown in weakness, raised in power;
sown a natural body, raised a spiritual body . . .

The first man was from the earth
and made of dust;
the second man is from heaven.
Like the man made of dust,
so are those who are made of dust;
like the heavenly man,
so are those who are heavenly.
And just as we have borne
the image of the man made of dust,
we will also bear
the image of the heavenly man.
1 Corinthians 15:12-14, 20, 35-37, 42-44, 47-49,
emphasis added

What do these Scriptures mean? What is a perfected body, and how do we pursue it? Paul had written to the church in Corinth to describe the firstfruits resurrection of the dead, the resurrection of people who died believing in Jesus Christ. He painted a picture, specifically, of what happens to the physical body after it dies. Painstakingly, he built a case and presented a structure of logic that arrived at this conclusion: If you are a believer in Christ, life is not over for you when you die. It is far from over. In fact, it is just beginning. If you believe that Jesus Christ rose from the dead, though your physical body may die, you will not remain dead. You will be changed.

Brothers, I tell you this: Flesh and blood cannot inherit the kingdom of God, and corruption cannot inherit incorruption. Listen! I am telling you a mystery:

> We will not all fall asleep,
> but we will be changed,
> in a moment, in the twinkling of an eye,
> at the last trumpet.
> For the trumpet will sound,
> and the dead will be raised incorruptible,
> and we will be changed.
> Because this corruptible must be clothed
> with incorruptibility,
> and this mortal must be clothed
> with immortality.
> When the corruptible is clothed
> with incorruptibility,
> and this mortal is clothed
> with immortality,
> then the saying that is written will take place:
> Death has been swallowed up in victory.
> 1 Corinthians 15:50-55

The day is coming when we will have, as William Shakespeare wrote, "shuffled off this mortal coil." This physical body is made of flesh and blood; it is full of corruption and it is mortal. It is weak and it is subject to illness, to pain and suffering, to abuse and sorrow, to frailty and death. Our physical bodies are not made of spiritual heavenly stuff and cannot inherit the Kingdom of God. They have not yet been perfected. Something supernatural needs to happen to transform our bodies of flesh and blood into bodies capable of experiencing the eternal life secured by the resurrection of Jesus Christ.

In Philippians 3:20-21, Paul further described the transition of the physical body into the perfected body this way: "But our citizenship is in heaven, from which we also eagerly wait for a Savior, the Lord Jesus Christ. He will transform the body of our humble condition into the likeness of His glorious body, by the power that enables Him to subject everything to Himself." In other words, our mortal, corruptible, physical bodies will be transformed "into the likeness of His glorious body," which is immortal and incorruptible.

One of the most beautiful things to me, when I ponder this upcoming transformation, is that we will not receive a completely new, unrecognizable body in order to inherit the Kingdom of Heaven. The one I have now will not be scrapped and replaced. *The body I have now will be transformed.* The body I have right now is no mistake. God gave it specifically to me. It makes me, *me*. It is not a subpar, inferior design choice. It was created in the image of God, it has been bought with a great price, and it is a seed; it is a deposit, a down payment of what is to come when death is swallowed up in victory.

The knowledge that my body is a vehicle doesn't diminish any of the glory that is to come. On the contrary, it enhances its value because it enables me to accurately define the standard by which I aspire to live. Perfected, not perfect. Every time I fight my flesh, the usurper, every time I put on a pair of pants that fit more snugly than they did before and wear them anyway, every time I walk in the sunshine and smile because it is a good day to be alive, every time I sacrifice the dreams I had of perfection, giving them up for the sake of the gospel, for the sake of cross, so that I can be like Him in His suffering, I am pursuing a perfected body. "My goal is to know Him and the power of His resurrection and the fellowship of His sufferings, being conformed to His death, assuming that I will somehow reach the resurrection from among the dead" (Philippians 3:10, niv).

Every decision I make, choosing the pursuit of a perfected body over a perfect one, I make in anticipation of the day mortality will be clothed in immortality.

At the time I am writing this, it is two weeks before Christmas. The tree is up and decorated, the halls have been decked, and the season of wonder is in full swing. I have the great privilege of being able to watch my children experience the thrilling anticipation of the coming holiday. There truly is nothing as magical as experiencing Christmas Day through the eyes of a little child. And Christmas Day is a wonderful day, indeed. But as I look back in time through the lens of my memory, I would have to confess that to me, even though Christmas Day was wonderful, Christmas Eve was the most wondrous day of all.

How well I remember (can you remember, too?) the night before Christmas. Stockings hung by the chimney with care, the cheerful fire in the fireplace slowly dying. It needed to be dark outside for Santa to come. He came under stealth and that required the dark, quiet hours of the night. Finally, the moment came to go to bed. But who could ever sleep on a night such as this? The air was electric with expectation. I lay in bed, straining to hear the sound of sleigh bells, the soft patter of reindeer hooves, my heart racing with excitement. Visions danced in my head—what would the tree look like tomorrow morning, alight and glowing, surrounded by a blanket of beautifully wrapped presents? The presents! What a thrilling thought! All the waiting, hoping, and good behavior, the mysterious winks and nods, would be brought to light and explained. The longing and wonder would culminate in a moment of glorious discovery.

Eventually, the sleepless hours of the long night ended and Christmas morning came. The presents were opened—I finally knew what those merry packages contained! And so the day passed. It was full of love and family and fun . . . but Christmas Day couldn't last forever. As the sun began to settle down in the west, the shadows grew longer and deeper, and I knew that wonderful day was drawing to a close. It was a thankful feeling, but it was also a sinking feeling, as the magic and the sparkle began to fade with the realization that Christmas was almost over. It was about to go away for a whole 365 days.

I suppose that is why I preferred Christmas Eve. It contained all the wonder of Christmas, but with endless magic, dreaming, and possibility. It was the night before the day that anything could happen. Christmas Day was wonderful—don't get me wrong—but it was over so quickly. It was so finite. Christmas Eve felt infinite.

Now we, the people with bodies made from the dust of the earth, who have put our faith in Jesus Christ, are but little children, dearly loved, barely able to sleep a wink in anticipation of the morning to come. What will it be like when we see Him face-to-face? What will it feel like, that first moment of breathless beholding, when the long, sleepless night is finally over? Darkness is rolled back and death is swallowed up in victory . . . Christmas Eve is over and Christmas Day dawns clear and bright. It is the real and living

Christmas. Its joy will never end. And my body will have been the vehicle that got me there, to that real and living Christmas Day. My body is the vehicle by which I came to find God and know Him in this world, experiencing the happiness and the sorrow and the heartache and the fight that is this life. This life, this Christmas Eve for the soul that puts its hope in Emmanuel Himself.

A perfected body is worth fighting for because Christmas Day is coming.

CHAPTER 15

Reformation

My tears are like the quiet drift
Of petals from some magic rose,
And all my grief flows from the rift
Of unremembered skies and snows.
I think, that if I touched the earth,
It would crumble;
It is so sad and beautiful,
So tremulously like a dream.

"CLOWN IN THE MOON," DYLAN THOMAS

QUESTION 6: Am I Using Food the Way God Intended?

The sound of a hammer striking iron into a wooden door reverberated throughout the quiet, rural town of Wittenberg, Germany, on October 31, 1517. With the hammer stroke of revolution Martin Luther nailed his 95 Theses to the door of Castle Church for all to see. He had written and presented a case against what he believed to be the egregious abuses of the papacy and the Catholic church, calling for a "'Disputation on the Power and Efficacy of Indulgences' out of love and zeal for truth and the desire to bring it to light."

At the time of this now renowned document, Martin Luther was a well-liked, but relatively obscure professor of theology at the

University of Wittenberg in a quiet hamlet in eastern Germany. He had been grappling with Scripture, attempting to reconcile what he read with the commonly accepted practices (the corrupt practices) of the Holy Roman Church. They appeared to be at odds with one another. It was this dichotomy, coupled with what he viewed as grave injustices perpetrated against the poor and feeble that propelled him to action. He nailed the 95 Theses to the door of the church in Wittenberg, and copies of it spread like wildfire across Europe. It would have certainly been impossible to foresee the great fire his words would spark, the fire of reformation that birthed the Protestant Church. It's a fire, that five hundred years later, is still blazing . . .

Martin Luther was born in Eisleben, Germany, in 1483. As a young man, he had originally studied law at the University of Erfurt. However at twenty-one, as he was traveling on the road to Erfurt, he encountered the mother of all thunderstorms and narrowly missed being struck by lightning. The experience shook him to the core, and in fear for his life he cried out, "Help me, St. Anne! I will become a monk!"

Luther followed through on his shadow of death declaration and became a monk. (Who can say no to God?) He was an exceptionally intelligent and driven individual; his devotion to the church proved no exception. Luther wholeheartedly engaged in all the monastic disciplines . . . he was on a quest to prove to God he was worthy of salvation. Yet despite his Herculean effort and works, and in spite of his good behavior, he harbored a monstrous fear—the wrath of a righteous God. He lived in constant fear of the terror of hell and the impending Judgment Day, unable to embrace any of the grace and mercy that he was told God offered penitent sinners.

The prevailing doctrines of the church reinforced this unrelenting fear: the papacy alone had the ability to interpret Scripture and was therefore the primary religious authority. Authority dictated that salvation was obtained through works. More specifically, forgiveness was received through this work: purchasing indulgences. An indulgence was a document issued by the church in exchange for payment. Someone who wanted to secure forgiveness for his own sins, or to release someone who had already died from purgatory, could buy an indulgence, thus freeing them or their loved one from eternal punishment. It was a seriously messed-up system that preyed upon the poor and the weak, who looked to the church for guidance and inspiration but instead were met with extortion. Commit a sin? No problem! For a small fee, with a tiny bit of penitence thrown in, you can be absolved forever!

But how could a person ever know if he had paid for all his wrongdoings? What if he accidentally did something and didn't realize he needed to pay for it? That thought haunted Luther. It was never enough. No amount of effort and striving and buying ever seemed to be enough. And yet, even in the midst of this, Luther managed to discover Christ. It was through his study of the book of Romans that Luther was able to say, "At last, by the mercy of God, meditating day and night, I . . . began to understand that the righteousness of God is that by which the righteous live by a gift of God, namely by faith. . . . Here I felt that I as altogether born again and had entered paradise itself through open gates."

He had a revelation of the good news of Jesus Christ. "For in it the righteousness of God is revealed from faith to faith, just as it is written: 'The righteous will live by faith'" (Romans 1:17).

This revelation inspired hope and freedom in Luther, but it also caused his eyes to be opened to the abuses of the church. At that very moment, the friar Johann Tetzel was on a campaign to sell indulgences, commissioned to do so by Pope Leo X himself, to finance St. Peter's Basilica in Rome. Tetzel's official title was "Grand commissioner for indulgences in Germany." The infamous claim he became synonymous with was, "Once a coin in the coffer clings, a soul from purgatory springs." Yes, this actually happened. At that moment in history it was absurdly easy to exploit the supernatural fears of the common populace. Fears the church itself had constructed. "Are thoughts of beloved, recently deceased Granny burning in agony in purgatory keeping you awake at night? Have I got a once-in-an-eternal-lifetime bargain for you! Purchase this onetime specially offered indulgence, and she will be freed!"

The blatant exploitation of grace for profit performed at the hands of the church finally aroused the wrath of Luther. He was incensed; he was truly and righteously angry, and that anger inspired him to put pen to paper and write the incendiary 95 Theses.

Does the practice of buying and selling indulgences remind you of anything? Have you ever overeaten and immediately felt like you needed to make up for it by being "extra good" the next day? Have you ever been overwhelmed with guilt and shame because you weren't able to follow through with your diet plan?

The church in Luther's day twisted the mercy of God, turning it into a mechanism by which they could make money, profiting off the exploitation of the misguided masses. The usurper uses our culture's obsessive and twisted views of food to attempt to wrest control from the one true living God. The flesh uses the fear of food—more specifically, fear of what happens to those who cannot control food—to accomplish this.

FOOD INDULGENCES

Thinking about food and talking about food can bring with it an enormous amount of emotional baggage. I have heard people describe it as their "drug of choice," their comfort, their weakness, their addiction, their Achilles' heel, their greatest love, and their greatest fear. Food is memories of a childhood home. It is failure when you have been trying so hard to be good. It is companionship in the darkness and loneliness. It is retribution when you deserve to be punished. That is quite a lot of power to ascribe to something that just lies there and can't move by itself.

Yet, food is very powerful. It is so powerful, that the mere mention of the word *spaghetti* has, in the past, been enough to cause me to fake an illness to avoid going to an event where I knew it would be served. Consuming pasta was one of the seven deadly nutritional sins. Nearly twenty years of my life was spent in abject terror and devotion to food. I planned my life's activities around the presence or absence of food. Its anticipated presence in a social situation would cause a chain reaction of thoughts within me . . .

What kind of food would be there? How much of it would be there? Would everyone else be eating the food? Would they expect me to eat the very same food they were eating? That's unacceptable. How could I possibly know the nutritional content of some random food item I did not personally prepare? How would they treat me when they noticed I was not eating the food? Would they say anything about it? Would they do anything about it?

This avalanche of thoughts caused overwhelming panic and despair. I knew, deep down, that though I tried with all my might to control my interactions with food, food was everywhere. It was only a matter of time before I would succumb to a moment of weakness and eat the wrong kind of food at the wrong time. And then what would I do?

I would have to find a way to atone for it.

The dread that Luther lived with, fear of a merciless God, was the fear I labored under as well. Only, in place of a vengeful God, I feared omnipresent and omnipotent food. In my wildest dreams, I could not picture a day when I would be a free and "normal" person when it came to food. Other people seemed to possess an ease of grace to exist and eat and drink and be merry, but I was the grotesque exception. Food was a shameful creation. It was an unfortunate and guilt-ridden necessity. How could loving God have done this to me?

The church of the sixteenth century was built on the backs of those so filled with guilt and shame, they would pay any price for relief from impending eternal torment. A culture of fear birthed an economy of indulgences that oppressed an entire continent. Today, the usurper has built an economy where the fear of being out of control and overweight is the hell that needs to be escaped from at any cost. We will pay anything.

How did we get here?

How did we become a society obsessed with food and body image?

Have you ever gone on a retreat for work, where two out of three meals were sumptuous affairs at restaurants, and determined that you would be extra good when you returned home to make up for it? Have you ever eaten cake at a birthday party and felt compelled to hit the gym extra hard to compensate? Have you ever looked at a particular food and said, "That food is bad" or "That food is good"? Have you ever done a cleanse in anticipation of seeing family members that you haven't seen for a year because you don't want them to realize you are a size bigger than last year? Have you ever dreaded an event because you knew there would be food there?

Our decision to use and manipulate food to find some measure of order in the chaos did not just spring up from the ground. We didn't wake up one morning and decide, "Being thin should be what society considers beautiful and important." The idea that food needs to be controlled and that controlling food, therefore being thin, is a positive thing, is far from a random revelation. It is a carefully constructed conspiracy, straight from the enemy.

Where did it come from? It came from our culture's obsession with being thin, and our culture is a product of prevailing beliefs.

These beliefs have a source. These beliefs have prophets and preachers and evangelists. They live to spread their false gospel. When I was in treatment, my nutritional therapist told me she had personal knowledge of a modeling agency that recruited specifically from eating disorder treatment centers. They literally were waiting to pounce the moment of discharge. Why? Girls with eating disorders were thin enough to be good models. Is being a model considered to be a positive or a negative thing in our society?

Have you ever browsed Pinterest, searching for health tips? Be prepared to be assaulted with thousands of images of what the picture of ideal health looks like. It doesn't matter which television shows you watch, which advertising you pass, which social media site you use . . . . all bow down to the preeminence of thinness. If you don't believe me, go to a middle school and ask a random sample of students if being thin is important. Ask them how it feels to be considered overweight. Ask them what makes someone appear attractive. If you want to get the true, unfiltered answer to the question "How important is being thin?" ask a middle schooler.

This monumental obsession with being thin opens the door for the usurper to sell his indulgences. Just like the church did in Martin Luther's day and for the same reasons.

"Are thoughts of being fat keeping you up at night? Have I got a once-in-a-lifetime deal for you! Control what you eat, lose weight, and then you'll be happy! Are thoughts of growing older and not being able to fit in your old clothes getting you down? Have I got the solution for you—plastic surgery, whole body cleanses, hours at the gym! Anything but growing older and bigger! Cut out sugar; that should do it! Didn't make you happy? Cut out carbs! Surely that will work. It didn't? Well, there are always prepackaged shakes and meals, since you obviously can't do this on your own! Did that do the job? Great! You were finally able to lose weight! Now you are happy!"

The usurper's campaign to sell indulgences intensifies once he realizes how absurdly easy it is to prey on your vulnerability and misguided beliefs. You bought one indulgence. Surely you will buy another. And another. And another. The cycle begins. Works, the extent to which you can properly control food, equal righteousness. And you buy and you buy indulgences, perhaps you sell them, too, until the day arrives when you realize the hamster wheel you have been on is going nowhere. *Nowhere.* Because controlling food works beautifully until it doesn't work anymore. Maybe you suffered an injury and can no longer exercise. Maybe you can't bear to drink another nutritional shake. Maybe you went on a vacation, and when you returned home, the willpower just wasn't there anymore. Controlling food worked until it didn't. And then you were left depressed, scrambling to discover the next revelation that would help you conquer your abuse of food, once and for all.

This cycle will continue until you have a moment of clarity, like Martin Luther did, and begin to understand you are no closer to happiness than when you first started the cycle. You realize you are sick and tired of participating in a system that props up a tyrant. That is why I always return to the same place. The usurper wants to be god. Think about it: If someone wanted to set himself up as a false god, he would need to establish an economy by which he could keep his subjects under his boot. An economy of behavior and rules whereby a subject could be determined a faithful disciple or a blasphemer. More often than not, the religious rule system the false king demands others live by is not the one he lives by, for he is above all and answers to no one. That is the natural right of a god. Gods exist for no one but themselves.

But make no mistake, there is only one God and His gospel brings freedom. His is an economy of grace that liberates the captives and sets the prisoners free.

THE BEGINNING OF A FOOD REFORMATION

The enemy has malicious schemes and we are not ignorant of them. The assault on our view of food employs a strategy straight from the Garden of Eden. It was and is this: to upend the natural order of something created by God to bring joy and happiness in its proper context. The serpent did this to Eve when he deceived her. The flesh wants to do the same to us. It wants us to believe food couldn't actually be a *good gift, given by a good Father.* It wants us to accept the lie that our Father must have played a trick on us; food is a disgusting and shameful necessity that needs to be militantly controlled.

The usurper cannot create; he possesses no original thoughts. He can only twist and distort the good gift God intended for our benefit. He preys on our moments of weakness and pain to peddle his cheap, imitation wares.

Maybe you were the little girl put on a diet.

Maybe you were the child who was rewarded with food, comforted with food, punished with food.

Maybe you were the boy who was mocked without mercy for the way you enjoyed eating food.

Maybe you were the young woman who was told, "You sure have a pretty face; it's too bad you eat so much."

Maybe you were the churchgoer told you needed to have more self-control. (It's a fruit of the spirit, didn't you know.)

Maybe you were the woman, who cried herself to sleep after bingeing, "Tomorrow, tomorrow, tomorrow, I will take control back." A plea to God...to herself.

No matter who we are, the usurper's end game is the same. He wants to indoctrinate us in order to drive us to a place we feel compelled to look to him for salvation, to buy indulgences from him in an attempt to atone for our calorific transgressions. That is what the flesh wants from us. It wants to dominate and destroy us. It uses food as the point of entry.

God intended something so much more for us in this beautiful, mundane, nourishing, satisfying, joyful, messy creation of food than the usurper could ever dream to offer. God intended for us to eat food because we were hungry, and the food tasted good; because we were lonely, and the act of sharing a meal brought us together; to eat food, having our fill, in order for us to understand the glorious mystery of life that has been lavished on us by a good Father.

The fight to reclaim the vision of food God intended thus becomes a knock-down, drag-out brawl to reconcile the truth against the inundation of lies. How can we do this? How can we obtain a more accurate view of what food was created to be? How do we stop the cycle of buying nutritional indulgences?

I would like to freely admit at this point I would never dare to attempt to spell out how to use food specifically. That is unique to each of us. The particulars of how I used food to restore my health might be very different from the way you need to use food to restore your health. We are all different; the ways we have abused food are many and varied. It would only stand to follow that the resolution of our diverse struggles would be equally diverse.

But before you begin to lament the fact that you have come this far along with me on this journey only to be disappointed that I am not going to tell you exactly what to do with food, I would like encourage you with the words of C. S. Lewis:

> Give up yourself, and you will find your real self. Lose your life and you will save it. Submit to death, death of your ambitions and favorite wishes every day . . . Nothing in you that has not died will ever be raised from the dead. Look for yourself, and you will find in the long run only hatred, loneliness, despair,

rage, ruin, and decay. *But look for Christ and you will find Him, and with Him everything else thrown in* (emphasis added).

Jesus promised, "But seek first the kingdom of God and His righteousness, and all these things will be provided for you" (Matthew 6:33). Believe me when I say that the details of what and how you should eat are indeed significant. God cares about this area of your life, because He cares about you. If we bring this area of our life to Him, in trust, prioritizing our relationship with God over our relationship with food, then the what and how of eating will be provided for us. So do not despair, because there is hope, real hope.

There are two guiding principles that can be a great help in fighting to reclaim a view of food that reflects what God intended. These principles will help you steer the course and keep your eyes on the Giver of all these things that He delights to add to us.

The first of the principles is this: Identify the lies you have believed about food and fight to counter them with the truth. Write your own 95 Theses and nail it to the front door! Let anger at the lies you have believed about food inspire you to revolutionary action. In the sixteenth century, it only took one little monk, a hammer, and a nail to start the fires of a reformation the likes of which the church had never seen since the time of Christ. It can be the same with us today. It takes strength to be a reformer. It takes vision to wake from the slumber of propping up an evil regime. It takes incredible daring to confront the lies of the culture and yell, "Knock it off!" It takes courage to disregard the lies of the usurper and live a life of reformation that declares, "Enough—this stops with me!"

It may seem like a simple enough thing to do. "Identify the lie and counter it with the truth." But simple does not always translate into easy. I understand as well as anyone that knowing something is true does not always translate into actually believing it to be true. Our dysfunctional feelings about food have been ingrained for a very long time, and they take a long time to unwind. It takes time spent practicing calling out lies and believing the truth. It also takes new perspective.

In the early stages of my own recovery, I felt that God gave me a prayer. Words to counter the lies at every meal in Jesus' name. I said this particular prayer before each meal, to confront lies with the truth: *God, thank You for this food. I am going to use this food the way You intended. I am going to use it for the nourishment of my body so that I will have the strength to do the work of Your Kingdom. Amen.*

Every meal. Every time I faced food. Praying that prayer on a routine basis was the first step for me. It was very helpful to have something practical to do when food was physically present in front of me.

If I had let myself think about all the meals that were to come, I would have bolted from the table and hidden under my covers. So I decided I would only think about the food I was going to be encountering the soonest. When I would sit down at the dinner table, I would tenaciously hang on to the longing in my soul to feel like a little girl again, to eat food that was provided for me out of love and care. The words of that prayer expressed the goal I had decided to pursue. It put into words the role I wanted food to play in my life, how I wanted to view food, helping me envision where I wanted to finally arrive at the end of this journey.

The second guiding principle in fighting to see food the way God intended is this: Mortality merits consideration. Today, as I sit here, my oldest daughter is seventeen years old. When I was in treatment, she was ten. Seven years have passed from the day I kissed her good-night in the darkness and left, not knowing if I would ever come home again. As you know by now, I did indeed come home. I have fought for my freedom and I have fought to have a life worth living. I am fighting today still.

My daughter is a very good volleyball player. She started to play a year after I returned home from treatment. This was a blessing beyond anything I could comprehend. I had loved playing volleyball so much and had given it up for the sake of the eating disorder when I was in college. I have been her coach, spending countless hours with her in the car to and from practices and tournaments. I am so thankful for this time. I believe with all my heart that God, in His love and mercy, gave a restoration of that experience back to me. And it is infinitely better, because I am able to enjoy watching one of my children love to do something that I loved to do. Not only does she love to play volleyball, she excels at it.

This fall was her senior volleyball season. The high school team she played on was very successful. They had won the state championship in North Carolina two years ago and were second in the state her junior year. Her senior year was shaping up to be very similar. As the season drew to a close, the team was, once again, undefeated in their conference. With the record of wins they had earned, they would be heading into the state tournament highly seeded. Things were looking bright; the team was doing well and Daisy was playing some of the best volleyball I had ever seen her play. Until . . . the coach tearfully told the girls that she had made a very big error. She had mistakenly played one of the junior varsity players in too many varsity matches, and the team was going to be forced to forfeit some of their wins, pay a fine, and would not be the conference champions.

The team was devastated. Not only were they stripped of the conference champion title, which they had earned, but they would now be seeded much lower in the state championship tournament. No more home court advantage. No more easy teams to play first. In this manner, the end of the season unfolded. They won their first round but had to travel three hours away to play a very highly ranked team in the second round.

As I sat there, watching this match, I was seething with anger at the chain of events that had transpired which had brought us to this moment in time. I could not believe this had happened to my daughter in her senior season. She deserved so much better. And the coach—the coach should have known better! She was no novice. There was no excuse for making such a rookie mistake.

The match was hard fought. It was very close, but the girls lost. I was livid her high school career had ended so unjustly. My anger persisted throughout a good portion of the evening. As the rage I had been feeling started to wane, I tried to mollify my feelings by convincing myself of the facts: It's just a game. You learn just as much from adversity as success. The coach feels terrible. She didn't do it on purpose. The girls did the best they could do. Daisy played great . . .

Yes. She had played great.

As the memory of the game turned over in my mind again, I began to feel sick. What had I been thinking? Why on earth had I been so angry? Who cares what happened? How could I have not realized I was watching my daughter play the last match of her high school career? How could I have not appreciated it for what it truly was? I would never be able to watch her play high school volleyball again. I shouldn't have sat there interpreting the night's events in anger and frustration. I should have sat back and drunk in the joy of the moment. I would never pass that way again. Ever.

The haunting poetic truth found in Ecclesiastes 12:1-8 reminds us:

Before the days of adversity come,
and the years approach when you will say,
"I have no delight in them";
before the sun and the light are darkened,

and the moon and the stars,
and the clouds return after the rain;
on the day when the guardians of the house tremble,
and the strong men stoop,
the women who grind cease because they are few,
and the ones who watch through the windows see dimly,
the doors at the street are shut
while the sound of the mill fades;
when one rises at the sound of a bird,
and all the daughters of song grow faint.
Also, they are afraid of heights and dangers on the road;
the almond tree blossoms,
the grasshopper loses its spring,
and the caper berry has no effect;
for man is headed to his eternal home,
and mourners will walk around in the street;
before the silver cord is snapped,
and the golden bowl is broken,
and the jar is shattered at the spring,
and the wheel is broken in to the well;
and the dust returns to the earth as it once was,
and the spirit returns to God who gave it.
"Absolute futility," says the Teacher. "Everything is futile."

Life goes by so very fast. That is what the writer of Ecclesiastes is conveying to us in this passage of Scripture. Those who were young are now old. All that was vibrant and industrious came to an end. At first blush, the author's conclusion, "Everything is futile," sounds horribly depressing. What is the use in living, in trying at all, if everything is meaningless? What is the use of building anything in this life when it will soon return to dust?

Yes, that certainly does sound demoralizing. But for those of us who have put our hope in Jesus Christ, the idea that life is fleeting is not depressing; it is sobering. It is a sobering thought to realize we have only a sliver of time here. Mortality merits consideration.

Indeed, the end is coming sooner than we could ever comprehend. If you are a parent, you see this truth played out in living color before your eyes every day. My youngest daughter, Rose, was two when I was in treatment. I used to sing her lullabies over the phone, "Roses love sunshine. Violets love dew. Angels in heaven know I love you." Now she is nine and goes around the house singing Adele's "Hello." Time marches on.

I can make a decision today regarding how I want to spend the rest of my life, my valuable, precious minutes of time. Do I want to spend my life buying and selling indulgences? Do I want to spend my life groveling before the usurper? Do I want to spend the remainder of my days interpreting life through the lens of futility? Or do I want to make a decision to fight for joy?

> There is nothing better for man than to eat, drink, and enjoy his work. I have seen that even this is from God's hand, *because who can eat and who can enjoy life apart from Him?*
> Ecclesiastes 2:24-25, emphasis added

Making a decision to fight for joy means deciding to believe that the ability to find enjoyment in food comes from God. Apart from God, the pursuit of seeing food correctly is pointless. The perspective through which you choose to see food makes all the difference in the world. It truly is the difference between embracing futility and embracing joy.

Deciding to fight for joy means putting food in its proper place, using it the way God intended. A. W. Tozer wrote, "The victorious Christian neither exalts nor downgrades himself. His interests have shifted from self to Christ." I don't think there could be a better description of what happens in regard to making a decision to reframe food. You don't make a decision to ignore or disregard food altogether and pretend it doesn't exist. Rather, you make a decision to shift your interests, regarding food, from yourself, from your own interests, to Christ's interests. Considering your mortality, with the gift of breath lent to you today, ask yourself, "How does God want me to use food? How does God intend for me to use food? How can I rely on God minute by minute, meal by meal, to choose joy over futility?"

Yes, life is fleeting and time is going by faster than we could ever imagine. But the same truth that governs the resurrection of the dead governs us, as we are now. As believers in Jesus Christ, the eternal is beginning now; now is the time for us to clothe ourselves in righteous anger and fight. If we listen closely enough, we may be able to hear the sound of a different 95 Theses being hammered to the front door of our generation for all to see. It has been written in the blood of the Lamb, absolving us forever. Nothing can be added to it. No amount of works or striving can change the fact that Jesus has made a way for us to see food differently. To see it as God intended. To use food as God intended. And to enjoy it.

CHAPTER 16

The Late Usurper

Promise smoldered inside him, like an ember.
KATHI APPELT

At what point does the usurper become the "late usurper"? When is the usurper dead and gone, nothing more than a forgotten memory? The definitive answer is when corruption has put on incorruption and mortality is clothed in immortality. Until that glorious transformation happens, the usurper, the flesh, will war against us with every ounce of strength it possesses, and we will war against it. If that is the case, then how do we quantify victory? If the total destruction of the flesh cannot be achieved until the day we are changed, in a moment, in the twinkling of an eye, how can we know we are winning in the here and now? What is the measurement of freedom?

There are two gauges I have found to be useful in quantifying how far I have come in my victory against the usurper.

PASSION

Let us lay aside every weight and the sin that so easily ensnares us,
and run with endurance the race that lies before us,
keeping our eyes on Jesus…

HEBREWS 12:1-2

The first gauge I call my passion gauge. It includes the six questions that I use to measure the extent of my passion to fight the usurper and his lies. I ask myself these questions every day.

1. Have I identified and declared war on the enemy?
2. Could I be happy if I never lost another pound or could never alter my physical appearance in any way?
3. Am I looking at the mirror inside as much as the mirror outside?
4. What am I doing with feelings that are too much to bear?
5. Am I pursuing a perfect body or a perfected body?
6. Am I using food the way God intended?

Hopefully you are beginning to understand that there are an infinite number of ways you can practice answering the questions, guided by the desire to please Him. We have come full circle back to where we first entertained the idea that the desire to please Him does in fact please Him. This desire, this passion, is paramount in making any kind of coherent progress in overthrowing the usurper. The desire to please Him is the North Star in the journey to victory. The questions provide both a starting point and an ending point in our fight against the usurper. If I ask myself, **"Have I identified the enemy?"** I have a place to stand and fight. I call the enemy out by name, and it's a point of departure. As I keep asking myself, "Have I identified the enemy?" I remain engaged in the process of concentrating my efforts in fighting against the right enemy, with the right end, its complete destruction, in mind. I declare war on the enemy, not on me. I don't waste valuable time and energy fighting against myself. I point every weapon I possess against the usurper and make sure those weapons remain trained on him. I discipline myself to ask these questions every single day because the enemy of my soul is relentless, and so I too must be relentless. I cannot afford to grow passive in my fight against the usurper.

In the same manner I daily ask myself, **"Could I be happy if I never lost another pound or could never alter my physical appearance in any way?"** I choose what is worth defending and will continue to fight with the end in mind. It's hard to decide to believe what seems to be unbelievable: that happiness exists apart from a change in my outward appearance. It's a battle that must be waged at the break of every dawn.

I continue to ask myself, **"Am I looking at the mirror inside as much as the mirror outside?"** understanding that doing this will reveal the deepest longing of my heart. It will give me the opportunity to offer that longing to my Father every day, asking Him to show me the revelation that will inspire the action I need to take to align my heart's desires with His.

"What am I doing with feelings that are too much to bear?" is a daily consideration on my heart and mind. I need to practice staying vulnerable with others, remembering that it's okay to give the unspeakable a voice and talk about my struggles out loud with another human being.

I ask myself every day, **"Am I pursuing a perfected body?"** because it redefines the standard by which I want to live. And I continue to ask the question, **"Am I using food the way God intended?"** in order to see through the deception of the enemy. To live a life where the joy of truth rises like a tide, overtaking the lies, redeeming the beauty of God's creation minute by minute.

This is a war; when an army's troops experience a loss in battle, they don't turn on themselves and wipe themselves out. They momentarily pause, assess what could have possibly gone wrong, regroup, restrategize, and relaunch a new strategic attack against the other side. When I continually keep these questions before me, I keep my sights focused on the advancement of my primary goal: victory at all costs.

The constant contemplation and practice of these questions serve as the mile markers in my fight for freedom. "Sobriety" is really tricky to define when one struggles with food issues. The questions in the "passion gauge" provide me a way to quantify my victories and successes, as well as warning shots across the bow if I am veering too far off the path to real freedom.

REPLACE THE USURPER

But Absalom, the man we anointed over us, has died in battle.
So why do you say nothing about restoring the king?

2 SAMUEL 19:10

The second gauge I have found to be helpful in quantifying victory over the usurper is the replacement gauge. Has the usurper's role in my life been replaced?

When I talk about replacing, I am not speaking of replacement in the usual sense. I am not saying, "Well, in the past when I was feeling alone and out of control, I would reach for my trigger food and inevitably end up doing what I didn't want to do. So now, when I am feeling alone and out of control, I will instead take a nice, long shower to get my mind off of it." That kind of replacement is helpful and serves a purpose, if the purpose and the goal are to change an outward behavior for the rest of my natural, physical life. That kind of "distracting behavior" is great for getting my mind off of wanting to act out, right here and right now. It works beautifully for behavior modification, temporally speaking.

The kind of replacement I am talking about is of an eternal nature. It replaces a life spent in captivity to the false king with a life spent in devotion to the one True King. It replaces the eating disorder with divine purpose.

When I sat as a seventeen-year-old girl with an unopened lunch, willing myself not to eat, I was looking for a king. The usurper presented its case: "I am the king you have been looking for. The real King doesn't know what He is doing. Give your allegiance to me." In a moment of unguarded shame and guilt, I believed the usurper.

We all need a king. Whether we know it or not, we cannot exist king-less. Every action we take is guided by our allegiance to the king we are serving. It might be a false king; it might be the True King. And there is a True King, make no mistake. But we all make a choice. As Bob Dylan put it, "You've gotta serve somebody."

In *Celebration of Discipline*, Richard Foster wrote:

> One of Israel's fatal mistakes was their insistence upon having a human king rather than resting in the theocratic rule of God over them. We can detect a note of sadness in the word of the Lord, "They have rejected me from being king over them" (1 Samuel 8:7). The history of religion is the story of an almost desperate scramble to have a king, a mediator, a priest, a pastor, a go-between. In this way we do not need to go to God ourselves. Such an approach saves us from the need to change, *for to be in the presence of God is to change* (emphasis added).

Only in the presence of God, the True King, can we really change. He is the King over every pretender, over every false king. His Kingdom brings freedom and divine purpose.

The false king leads me into bondage. The True King snaps chains. The false king, the usurper, traps me in a labyrinth of lies. The True King crushes lies with the light of truth. The usurper promises to set me free from shame. The True King ushers in a life of everlasting freedom. The eating disorder promises that I can find love and peace and meaning and value. The True King delivers all of those things and so much more. The True King replaces the old pattern of disordered behavior and death with glorious, radical fire, burning away every trace of what used to hold me in deadly captivity.

The True King replaces the eating disorder with divine purpose.

Can you imagine it? Real, eternal, divine purpose? Divine purpose like the great heroes of the Bible had. Divine purpose compelled Daniel to throw open his windows and pray aloud, "as was his custom" (Daniel 6:10, nkjv), knowing full well that he would be thrown into the lions' den for doing so. Divine purpose gave Queen Esther the courage to steel herself against fear and go before the king to plead the case against horrific injustice, confident that she was brought "to the kingdom for such a time as this" (Esther 4:14, nkjv). Divine purpose emboldened a boy named David to stand with only a sling and few small stones against a giant.

Divine purpose paints every picture with the perspective of eternity. Divine purpose whispers to me in the dark moments of the soul, comforting me with what really matters. Divine purpose is a woman set free from the tyranny of a distorted body image. Divine purpose is "I have been crucified with Christ and I no longer live, but Christ lives in me. The life I now live in the body, I live by faith in the Son of God, who loved me and gave Himself for me" (Galatians 2:19-20).

I used to believe that living a life of divine purpose was an illusion. That kind of recovery, to me, was a mirage. Hadn't I always been believed that I would have to deal with "disordered eating," in some form or another, for the rest of my life? That I would be forever tormented by calories and sizes, by nightmares of double chins and thighs rubbing together? That I would forever be haunted by the judgements of other people who deemed me lazy because I was no longer fit and trim? Hadn't I always been convinced, beyond any doubt, that the promise of complete freedom was a falsehood designed to string me along? One more step, one more step, one more step—the promise of freedom was the carrot at the end of the stick compelling me onward, tricking me into believing that a life of freedom was waiting for me, just a bit farther ahead. But I knew better.

Sure, I believed it was possible to recover insofar as I wasn't actively acting out my eating disorder. But to recover and not care about what I weighed? Not care about what I ate? Not care what others thought of me, based upon what I weighed and what I ate, whether it was too much or too little? That was a dream and it seemed too good to be true.

But dreams are worth fighting for.

For three years I fought. For three years I labored, practicing answering the six questions. For three years I stopped the eating disorder behavior altogether. Yet despite doing this, despite experiencing victory, I still harbored the monstrous fear that the grand illusion of complete freedom and recovery was just that—an illusion. I had come so far but was still so empty. I had overthrown the false king but I was still struggling, trapped in a vicious cycle of discouragement.

I've done all of this hard work, and I don't want to have an eating disorder anymore. It ought to be easier than this by now. Why I am I still struggling? Why do I still feel so empty? Why do I still care about what I weigh? I don't want to care about what I weigh!

In the midst of a spectacular relapse (yes, I have relapsed more times than I care to count), I had a moment of epiphany. I realized if I wanted true and lasting freedom, to eat because I was hungry and the food tasted good and it gave me energy to get through my day with joy and zeal, then I had to do something revolutionary. I couldn't merely live in the empty void of simply living life without an eating disorder, of living a usurper-less life. I had to replace the usurper with the rightful King and allow the life-giving divine purpose His Kingdom brings to fill my life. Every part of me—filled and overflowing with divine purpose.

For you see, divine purpose isn't a set of rules and regulations to follow. It's not a belief in a system; it's a belief in a person. It's not a formula; it's faith.

THE SON OF THE LIVING GOD

In Matthew 16:13-18, Jesus asked His disciples this question:

"Who do people say the Son of Man is?"

And they said, "Some say John the Baptist; others, Elijah; and still others, Jeremiah, or one of the prophets."

"But you?" He asked them, "who do you say that I am?"

Simon Peter answered, "You are the Messiah, the Son of the living God."

And Jesus responded, "Simon son of Jonah you are blessed because flesh and blood did not reveal this to you, but My Father in heaven. And I also say to you that you are Peter, and on this rock I will build My church, and the forces of Hades will not overpower it."

With this exchange, Jesus gave Simon a new name. Peter. Jesus told the newly called Peter he was a rock, upon which He was going to build His church. All this was true, and was possible, because Peter chose to see Jesus as the Messiah, through the eyes of eternal perspective.

Jump ahead in time . . . it is a matter of hours after the resurrection. Peter is standing before a risen and victorious Savior, who is asking him yet another question.

Jesus asked Simon Peter, "'Simon . . . do you love Me . . . ?"

"Yes, Lord," he said to Him, "You know that I love you."

"Feed My lambs," He told him.

A second time He asked him, ". . . do you love Me?"

"Yes, Lord," he said to Him, " You know that I love You." . . .

He asked him the third time, ". . . do you love Me?"

Peter was grieved. . . . He said, "Lord, You know everything! You know that I love you."

John 21:15-17

It was painfully obvious to Peter. Jesus knew Peter had denied him three times very publicly, when all hope seemed lost, the crucifixion of Jesus an imminent reality. Jesus knew the full extent of Peter's treachery. In that moment He needed Peter to fully understand the depth of it and acknowledge it. It was as if Jesus said, "Let's get this out of the way once and for all. I know who you are and what you are capable of doing. I know your flesh and all your deepest failings. I know all your hurts, all your fears, and all your shame. But do not be mistaken—I am still going to build My church on you, and the gates of hell will not prevail against it."

How we answer the two great questions **"Who do you say that I am?"** and **"Do you love me?"** changes everything. A. W. Tozer wrote, "What comes into our minds when we think about God is the most important thing about us." It takes eyes that see beyond flesh and blood to recognize Jesus Christ for who He is. He is the True King. This is no small thing. It is everything. If you can answer these two great questions with the responses, "I believe You are the Christ, the Son of the living God, the True King, building an eternal Kingdom of sacrificial love and divine purpose," and "Yes, Lord, I do love You," your life will never be the same. Whether in suffering or ease, your purpose and perspective will be radically redefined.

In John 11, Jesus interacted with a woman named Martha. The circumstances of this conversation were not happy. Lazarus, the brother of Martha and her sister, Mary, had died an untimely death four days prior to Jesus's arrival.

> Martha said to Jesus, "Lord if You had been here, my brother wouldn't have died. Yet even now I know that whatever You ask from God, God will give You."
>
> "Your brother will rise again," Jesus told her.
>
> Martha said, "I know that he will rise again in the resurrection at the last day."
>
> Jesus said to her, "I am the resurrection and the life. The one who believes in Me, even if he dies, will live. Everyone who lives and believes in Me will never die—ever. Do you believe this?"
>
> "Yes, Lord," she told Him, "I believe You are the Messiah, the Son of God, who was come into the world."

Fascinating.

Martha believed in the resurrection of the dead, as was the prevalent Jewish teaching. She did not hesitate to affirm to Jesus that she believed her brother would indeed rise again. Some day. But there was Jesus, telling her He was the resurrection. Judas hadn't handed Jesus over to the Jewish authorities yet. Nor had the Roman Empire crucified Him. He hadn't died and, after His death, been resurrected from the dead. How could He possibly call Himself the resurrection at that moment, standing in front of Martha, in sight of her dead brother's grave?

Jesus *is* the resurrection and the life. Not just of bodies that are dead in the ground, waiting to be clothed in immortality, but of all that we see and experience now.

> But God, who is abundant in mercy, because of His great love that He had for us, made us alive with the Messiah even though we were dead in trespasses. By grace you are saved! He also

raised us up with Him and seated us with Him in the heavens, in Christ Jesus, Together with Christ Jesus so that in the coming ages He might display the immeasurable riches of His grace in His kindness to us in Christ Jesus.
Ephesians 2:4-7

This Scripture tells me everything I need to know about what death and life and eternity mean to me as I fight against the usurper, the flesh, in the here and now. It tells me a perfected body is indeed on its way, and the time is coming when all wrongs will be put right, and we will fully understand what was actually wrong and why it needed to be put right. That day is coming. The empty tomb declares it. But resurrection is also in the here and now because Jesus is the resurrection and the life. He overwhelms our deadness with His life.

You see, Lazarus did not stay dead in his tomb. Things that are dead have a habit of coming alive when they collide with the Messiah, the Son of the living God, the Resurrection. That is why the way we answer the two great questions "Who do you say that I am?" and "Do you love me?" makes all the difference in the world.

Jesus *is* the True King.

BY THIS LIGHT I NOW SEE

One day, not too long ago, I woke up in the pale half-light of early morning. I stumbled around, rubbing my eyes, and walked over to the window. When I opened the window, the crisp fragrance of fall came flooding in. The leaves on the trees danced slightly in a soft breeze. I breathed deeply as the sun rose in a steady pink glow, the edge of the horizon rimmed in fire. The world was waking up.

I went about my morning doings—fixing hair and packing book bags, making sure every piece of homework was done and that the violin would not lie forgotten on the kitchen table. I got dressed and readied myself to face my own day. That evening, I went to one of my daughter's volleyball games, and I cheered and chatted and relished every moment. I got in the car with my daughter, enjoying the steady stream of conversation about the happenings of the day. We pulled up in front of our house. Our home. And I gasped with disbelief. I hadn't thought about my weight all day.

And I hadn't even tried to *not* think about it.

Talk about divine purpose! In that moment of realization, a crashing wave of thankfulness engulfed me. I was finally an example worthy of my children. The fire of eternal purpose, which was but an ember, burst into brilliant flame. I couldn't believe that it was really happening to me. The fire was burning "me" away. And before me, life was nothing but endless possibility. Before me was life that I had never dreamed possible.

It was life without an eating disorder.

The eating disorder had been replaced. And let me tell you, the moment I realized life without an eating disorder was possible was tantamount to the first sight of the man born blind from birth. "One thing I do know: I was blind, and now I can see!" (John 9:25). It was a moment equal to the storming of the beaches at Normandy. The enormity of a twenty-year struggle with an eating disorder flashed before me, and hope seized me so violently I began to shake. I saw myself as a seventeen-year-old girl in a schoolroom with an unopened lunch, willing herself not to eat, and I spoke to her.

"Don't do it!"

I knew full well nothing would change for her. The sad story of her life with an eating disorder would unfold. And it would indeed be sad; it would be filled with heartache and hurt and pain and disappointment. She would be sick; she would let down people who loved her; she would be ashamed of herself, and others would tell her she should be ashamed of herself. She would live in the shadow of all the what-ifs and the if-onlys, and she would pray to God above, "One day, please, one day, let this all make sense."

As I sat there in the car, I felt God wrap His infinite arms around that seventeen-year-old girl, around me, and all those moments in time came down to one moment in time and I began to cry; I cried as a little girl laying her head on her Father's chest, safely encircled in His arms. I felt as if the God of heaven and earth wiped my tears away, collecting them in a bottle. My heart whispered to Him, "Believe me when I say, my life has been, and always will be yours, God."

Now, as all of this had been going on with my daughter sitting in the car with me, I felt that I had some explaining to do. She looked at me with loving concern. "Are you okay?" Before I could begin to answer, she said, "I know. I feel the same way, too. It's good to be home. It's been a long day."

I'm here to make an audacious promise to you. If you replace your eating disorder with the consuming fire of divine purpose, dedicating your life in service to the True King, whose law brings life, you will be free. And everything that makes up your life as you now know it, the lovely and the unlovely, will become fuel to feed the fire of divine purpose.

The missionary Amy Carmichael penned the words of this poem:

> *From silken self, O Captain, free*
> *Thy soldier who would follow Thee.*
> *From subtle love of softening things*
> *From easy choices, weakenings,*
> *(Not thus are spirits fortified,*
> *Not this way went the Crucified . . .)*
> *Make me Thy fuel, Flame of God.*

It may not happen the next day or the next week or the next month. You may begin to doubt and waver as you daily feed the fire of divine purpose, as you passionately practice answering the questions. But the day is coming when you will realize it has been a while since you have listened to, or even heard, the voice of condemnation in your head. You haven't been able to hear it over the sound of laughter or the melodies of life that have been echoing in its place—for the True King is on the throne. When that day comes, divine purpose will ignite in your soul in glorious flame, and you will know, beyond any doubt, you will never be the same.

CHAPTER 17

The Beginning

And then I said, "Look at the moon." And he did. We just stood there until the sun was down and the moon was up. They seemed to float on the horizon for quite a long time, I suppose because they were both so bright you couldn't get a clear look at them. And that grave, and my father, and I, were exactly between them, which seemed amazing to me at the time, since I hadn't given much thought to the horizon.

My father said, "I would have never thought this place could be beautiful. I'm glad to know it."

GILEAD, MARILYNNE ROBINSON

Hope—real hope—is a powerful thing. In August 2012, almost three years from that dark and redemptive day when I laid bare my soul to that Sunday morning congregation, declaring war on the usurper, I found myself standing on a different platform altogether. I was at Saddleback Church, at the Celebrate Recovery Summit, sharing my testimony.

The crowd was vast; it was an assembly of thousands and thousands of people whose lives had been redeemed and made new. Words still fail me when I attempt to describe that moment in time. It was the culmination of years of agony and despair and hoping and failing and hoping again and failing again and work—

lots and lots of hard work—and the dawning of a brand-new day, bright and shiny with endless possibility. As I stood there, I was no longer shrinking away in shame and condemnation, feeling like I was somehow not a part of what was happening to me anymore. I felt brave and fierce, drinking in every moment, every sound, every emotion. There were thousands of faces in that crowd, looking at me expectantly, wishing to rejoice with me when I rejoiced and mourn with me when I mourned. Love was so real in that place, and it was beautiful to behold; it was the kind of love that beautified everything around it, making everything lovelier for having been in its presence.

It was in the magnificence of that place which love had made beautiful I shared the story of my pain and failure. I started at the beginning, when I was a little girl. How I became scared and began to lose my way. And when the heartache and struggle and the managing and doing of life became too intense, how I pledged myself to the usurper. How I became a slave to the eating disorder, to my flesh. How I was slowly crushed by a weight that was too heavy to bear, suffocated by living in secret degradation. Finally how I reached the end of my own hoarded resources and told someone. Well, actually, I told *everyone*. I continued sharing how I identified the enemy and made a decision to fight—to fight with violence. But the fields of battle did not miraculously clear, and the adversary I was fighting against was devious and unwavering, and I lost many battles along the way and I wanted to surrender.

But I did not surrender.

The fighting became intense, the outcome seemed hopeless, and victory seemed unattainable. I began to comfort myself with reincarnated lies, such as "This is just the way it is going to have to be, I suppose." But then I remembered I had put my faith in the Son of God, who loved me and gave Himself up for me, and because of this, the eternal is now. And the moment was coming, which no eye has seen and no ear has heard, when my body, which had been a good and faithful vehicle, would be changed. Mortality would be clothed in immortality, and *that* was worth fighting for. I told them how I made daily decisions to keep being vulnerable, to share my emotions, both the lovely and the unlovely, with another human soul. I made amends to those I harmed, my husband being the first person. Although I had not yet attained perfection, the old desires and the purpose my life had clung to were being replaced by new desires; glorious, eternal purpose was transforming me and my entire family.

By the grace of God, I testified, the usurper was being overthrown!

Sharing my testimony at Saddleback was truly a dream come true. Honestly, it was something I never could have predicted would happen to me, even in the wildest of fantasies. It was only possible because some truly fantastic people, who I could never adequately thank in this life here on earth, believed in me when I could not believe in myself. Their friendship and support blindsided me with blessings. Having experienced this undeserved opportunity to give my testimony, I have vowed to live a life worthy of such an opportunity.

I suppose that is the nature of redemption. It is completely undeserved—who could ever deem what is an adequate response? It is also the nature of recovery—real and genuine recovery. We stop trying to make others believe that we are worthy, and we begin to live a life that aspires, at every moment, to *be* worthy. Who then could ever possibly say when that standard has been met? When are we given our discharge papers, stamped 100 percent recovered? When can we say, "And they lived happily ever after" or "They rode off into the glorious sunset"?

Robert Farrar Capon describes the nature of the yearning to live a life in keeping with the great grace we have been given like this:

But all the while, the one thing we needed most even then—and certainly will need from here on out into the New Jerusalem— was the ability to take our freedom seriously and act on it; to live, not in fear of mistakes, but in the knowledge that no mistakes can hold a candle to the love that draws us home. My repentance, accordingly, is not so much for my failings but for the two-bit attitude toward them by which I made them more sovereign than grace. Grace—the imperative to hear the music, not just listen for the errors—makes all infirmities occasions of glory.

I was familiar with these "occasions of glory" in the days that followed me sharing my testimony. I know what it feels like to wake up the day after giving my testimony at the Summit. I know what it feels like to go back to the Summit, a year later and see the same people. "Your testimony really inspired me!" they would tell me. I know what it feels like to stand before those wonderful, kind people and feel the sinking dread in the pit of my stomach, knowing I could not possibly be living up to their lofty assessment of me. I know what it feels like to stand before a closet of too-small clothes and cry. I know what it feels like to look into the mirror and tell myself, "Who do you think you are? All those people think you are set free. I know who you really are. You cried about having to go to that wedding where people were going to see that you aren't thin and in control anymore."

Yes, I know what it is like to relapse.

Relapse has all the features of a four-letter word. It is the dark terror waiting to ambush us in the night. I am intimately acquainted with it. I used to wear the shame of relapse like Jacob Marley's chains. It was obvious to everyone that I was still struggling; they were aware of my many failings. Their awareness convinced me I deserved the chains of relapsing so often and so publicly. But victory isn't defined by how often we have failed; it is defined by how many times we get up and try again. I frequently describe my story as falling down 1,000 times and getting up 1,001. I would be very proud if that is the legacy I could pass on to you. Never give up.

I also I know what it is like to cry about all of my too-small clothes that will never fit again, and still boldly proclaim, "It doesn't matter! For I will be changed, in a moment, in the blink of an eye! [This] one thing I do: Forgetting what is what is behind (and that includes all of my too-small clothes) and . . .reaching forward to what is ahead, I pursue as my goal the prize promised by God's heavenly call in Christ Jesus" (Philippians 3:13-14).

Because, as Robert Farrar Capon also wrote, "We were never told that it would not hurt, only that nothing would ever finally go wrong; not that it would not often go hard with us but that *There is therefore now no condemnation to them which are in Christ Jesus.*"

I know what it is to fight, to mutinously oppose the condemnation of the eating disorder, the usurper, violently countering lies with eternal truth. I have trained myself to practice the questions, to wage war against the usurper with the force of heaven, with the Word of God. With real, living Truth. The Truth: I am choosing to live this way. I am choosing to use food the way God intended because I want to be happy, and I want to live a life worthy of emulation. I want to be a woman my daughters can look to for guidance. I don't want to be a slave to the usurper and its desires.

The usurper, the flesh, is a liar. It is a fraud, a charlatan wholly impotent to deliver anything of value. The best it can do is take something altogether beautiful and true and warp it into something shameful. Perhaps one of the most tragic things I allowed the usurper to convince me of was that the church was a place of condemnation. When I was finally healthy and could aptly discern the truth, I was able to see the depths of this deception and discover what the church really is. Yes, the church can be a place where some misguided people, on their own quest to find fulfillment apart from the grace of God, devise a religious system whereby they can feel superior. Yes, the church can be a place filled with hypocrisy. Yes, it can be a place that demands perfection—putting works on a scale and measuring them against arbitrary standards of righteousness. Yes, the church can often be a poor reflection of the Light of the World.

What does that have to do with the Truth?

The church was God's idea. It is His bride. It is His body. It is of infinite and eternal worth. And the gates of hell can never prevail against it. The church is a place full of people—people who struggle, fail, falter, and despair; who walk alone, experience sickness and tragedy, heartbreak and hurt; who succeed, prevail, triumph, and lift others up; who experience healing and victory, restoration and forgiveness; who overcome by the blood of the Lamb and the word of their testimony. The Son of God loves these people. He gave Himself up for them.

Today, I choose to reject the distorted, cheap, imitation reality the usurper would have me believe the church is. I have decided that loving something involves risk—but it is a risk I will gladly take—and I love the church. I really do. Celebrate Recovery, and the grace I found there, played an immeasurable role in helping me fall in love with the church, seeing it through the eyes of eternal perspective.

Sometimes change comes in an instant, with shock and awe. Sometimes it comes quietly, like a planted seed growing. It is a fact of nature that what has been sown, given the right conditions, will grow and mature. Though at times, the "right conditions"—the rains that push thoughts of sunshine into distant memory—can appear bleak. But often the way things appear have nothing to do with the way they really are. For rain is necessary for healthy things to grow. Pain can be equally necessary.

In such a way, my church hurt was necessary, and I am thankful for it. Without it I would have never grown into health and discovered the richness of the fellowship and discipleship I found in Celebrate Recovery. Pain drove me to a place where I was forced to search for real and living wholeness, never settling for the forgery of life the usurper would have me accept. If not for the "right conditions," I would have always believed that what church people said about me was a reflection of what God thought of me. I would have never understood that what people thought of me, whether it was positive or negative, could never hold a candle to what God *did* for me, to Truth.

BUILT ON A ROCK

All of this Truth is a choice; it is my choice to believe it or not. I can decide to build my life on it or not. And those daily decisions about what I believe are how I continue to win this war and overthrow the usurper. What I do will follow very closely after what I believe. This is true for good as well as evil.

> Therefore, everyone who hears these words of Mine and acts on them will be like a sensible man who built his house on the rock. The rain fell, the rivers rose, and the winds blew and pounded that house. Yet it didn't collapse, because its foundation was on the rock. But everyone who hears these words of Mine and doesn't act on them will be like a foolish man who built his house on the sand. The rain fell, the rivers rose, the winds blew and pounded the house, and it collapsed. And its collapse was great!
> Matthew 7:24-27

It is not enough to merely hear Truth. We must put it into action in order to build the kind of house that will weather any storm. Because the rains will come. The rivers will rise. The winds will blow and pound.

This winter, my husband, my daughters, and I traveled to Duluth, Minnesota, to spend Christmas with family. Duluth is situated on the shores of Lake Superior, the largest of the Great Lakes. If you have never seen a Great Lake before, it is hard to imagine how a body of water so vast could be considered a lowly lake. It is positively immense. We were staying in a cozy, historic home (circa 1886), directly on the beach, in sight of the Aerial Lift Bridge, rising and lowering to allow the enormous freight ships, which travelled as far as Russia, access to the harbor. Our house had a second-story porch, and if you walked to the edge of it, it seemed as though you were over the waters themselves.

Christmastime in Minnesota is a pretty cold affair. It was beautiful, make no mistake, but it was frigid, the kind of cold that took your breath away and shocked the senses with numbing alacrity. It was so cold, the waters of Lake Superior itself were covered with chunks of ice reminiscent of a prehistoric age, gently drifting in the ebb and flow of the normal rhythms of the lake.

Christmas night, the winds began to change. The surface of the lake was no longer serene. I could feel the shift in the weather, as I sat wrapped and warm inside our homely rental house, surrounded by the shrapnel of the day's activities. (Gift opening and making merry are very enthusiastic endeavors, after all.) The howling of the wind mingled with the sharp-metallic-crystalline sound of ice hitting the windows of the house; the house seemed to groan as the wind wailed against it. It was a disconcerting feeling, knowing that the house we were staying in had been built on the tenuous divide, between land and Great Lake, perched on the precipice. It felt entirely unsafe.

I wondered what kind of a person had put hammer to nail to compose this house, board by board, all those years ago. Was it a sailor? A ship's Captain? Did his wife look out of the very same ice-encrusted windows that I was now looking out of, waiting for her husband to return from the other side of the world? When he came home, did he grab his children up in his arms? Did they nuzzle their faces in his frosty beard? Did they look out over the same churning black waters on Christmas night and whisper a prayer for the safety of every soul who, like their father, was out there, somewhere, voyaging through the great beyond?

As I pondered these questions, I was seized with the desire to venture out to see, with my own eyes, what exactly was happening to the Great Lake Superior; to feel the storm as it bore down with primal intensity; to imagine the weight of the ages of the storms that had broken upon these frozen shores. I walked onto the second-story porch, to the very edge, and leaned forward as far as I dared to feel as though I were hovering over the waters.

Darkness stretched out over the face of the lake; the feeling of absolute night swallowed the lake whole. I could see nothing but ink-soaked darkness, nothing but the savage advancing of the white-tipped waves, which were growing larger by the minute, as an ice storm blew in on an unseen arctic wind. I could feel nothing but the wind. Wind and ice. It was such an unnerving feeling, standing at the edge of a wild abyss. I was frightened, taken aback by the awesome power of the wind and water. I was stunned at the immensity of the crashing blackness, where the water met the sky. (Or did the sky meet the water?)

Though mostly, I felt thankful. Thankful I was safe and secure. Lodged in a house that had stood the test of time, through more than a hundred winters, more than a thousand storms.

Choosing to act on the Truth is like that. Though the winds rage and the waters rise, it is the safe place to stand; it is safe because its foundation is the rock. The cold dread of a storm may break on us, threatening to tear apart the Truth we have fought so hard to build our lives on, but it can never prevail. We have built our lives on choosing Truth. The usurper is utterly powerless in the face of such an action of faith.

In James 2:26 we read, "Faith without works is dead." Yes, that is absolutely true. It takes an indescribable amount of faith to tell our flesh, every day, to go to hell. Which, incidentally, is where it has been trying to take us. The kind of faith that leads to victory isn't only found at the altar of a church; it is found in the mundane act of putting a fork to our mouths and thanking the Creator for the creation of food, in taking a deep breath while we are out for a walk instead of counting the calories we have burned, in feeling repulsed and ashamed of how we look and going out anyway.

It takes faith to bow our heads and pray before every meal, "Lord, thank You for this food."

Recently, I was sitting in the front row of church at a Sunday morning service. It was an inspirational sermon, full of the power of the Holy Spirit and emotional fervor. As someone who has been deeply hurt by a church in the past, I pride myself on eschewing my previous churchy habits and behaviors. For example, I never sit in the same seat twice. This is a reaction to a harrowing incident involving "assigned seating" when I unwittingly sat in a family's personal row of chairs. That Sunday morning I found myself, for the first time in a long time, up close to the location of the altar. (But where is the altar, really?) In response to the powerful message I had just heard, I felt compelled to go up and pray and pour my heart out to God. I felt the sensation of starting to lunge forward but quickly stopped myself from performing such a spectacle. I suppose to the outside observer, I looked like I had just experienced some sort of Pentecostal malfunction.

This is what was happening inside of my head at that exact moment: I had indeed felt the drawing power of God to go up and pray and worship God at the altar. However, I have a form of PTSD in regards to going up to the altar in front of other people, as this was the location of some of the deepest episodes of condemnation ever perpetrated against me, by others and by myself. So I stopped myself short. My thoughts began to revert to the old pattern of thinking: *I can't bear to go up there and publicly beg God to heal me, because I know it is hopeless.* In a visceral reaction to the experience, panic and fear were beginning to inundate my senses.

Then Truth came down upon me, strong as a mighty rushing wind. It spoke blessed assurance, "You have been healed."

I began to shake. I had been healed! Yes, my healing hadn't happened in one sweeping wave of instantaneous miraculous transformation. I had fought and toiled and believed for my healing every moment of every day of the past five years. And if *that* isn't a miracle, then I don't know what is. I stood at the threshold of that altar with utter certainty I was healed. Really and truly set free. I had indeed been transformed by the renewing of my mind. I fell before God at that much misunderstood and previously abused altar, and I was overcome with joy and wonder at the knowledge of the character and the majesty of God. And filled to overflowing with thankfulness, plain and simple, for the marvelous thing He had done for me and was now using me to do for others.

Time is a remarkable thing. It measures our days, the very essence of our existence as we move from the beginning to the end. It is the mechanism by which we can see how much things have changed, how much things have moved, how irrevocably events have shaped us and molded us into what we have become. We are travelers here, in this world that we can see with our two eyes. Time charts our journey.

I remember the day in November 2009, through the lens of time, sitting on a filthy brown couch in a treatment center in the desert. There was a battle cry in my heart. *"No one can make me do what I don't want to do!"* It was a battle cry borne of shame, resignation that I would forever be a slave to the eating disorder.

I also remember the day in December 2009, during family week, when my husband looked at me, at the *real* me, and told me I was worth fighting for, that I was not the eating disorder, that the usurper was a damnable adversary, that together we would fight to the bitter end. I uttered a new battle cry. *"I will fight a righteous fight for freedom. Whatever happens, whatever becomes of me, I will fight!"*

Today, as I turn back the pages of time, to observe where I have been in order to determine where I want to go, I see that my life has always been a battle cry. I spent many years—too many years—warring against myself. I will do so no longer. I will dedicate the violence of my efforts into overthrowing the usurper. I will endeavor to begin a new conversation: one where physical appearance has *nothing* to do with value. Nothing. The physical standards this society demands we judge ourselves against are patently wicked. They are false. They are constructs specifically designed by a false king to wrest life-giving power from the one true God. They exchange the truth of God for a lie. I reject them. I invite you to reject them, too. This is my new battle cry: *"Enough! This stops with me! For I shall be changed, in a moment, in the twinkling of an eye!"*

By faith he [Abraham] sojourned in the land of promise, as in a foreign land, living in tents with Isaac and Jacob, heirs with him of the same promise. For he looked forward to the city which has foundations, whose builder and maker is God.
Hebrews 11:9-10, rsv

In *The Fellowship of the Ring*, Tolkien wrote, "All that is gold does not glitter, not all those who wander are lost."

So I, like Abraham and countless sojourners before me, am a looker and a wanderer. We all are, all of us who have decided to make living with eternal perspective the only thing worth fighting for. James 4:14 tells us, "You don't even know what tomorrow will bring—what your life will be! For you are a bit of smoke that appears for a little while, then vanishes." It is remarkable to me, that this knowledge, that all I am experiencing now, all I can see with my eyes, is momentary and fleeting, is not a depressing knowledge. On the contrary, it is immensely comforting. It is supremely consoling, that if I can fight this good fight, with violence and divine purpose, in the end, there will be an End. And every echo of happiness I thought I had ever heard will be swallowed up in the resounding anthem of "It is finished" (John 19:30).

At the End of it all, which is really just the Beginning, if I were somehow given the chance to undo the chain of events and choices that would form the wreckage of my life with an eating disorder, maybe I would. But I don't think I really would. Because what is behind me is nothing, *nothing*, compared to what is before me.

Epilogue

At night I love to listen to the stars.
It is like five hundred million little bells.

"THE LITTLE PRINCE," ANTOINE DE SAINT-EXUPÉRY

There is a stretch of cultivated fields along winding country roads that intersect adjacent to my daughter's redbrick elementary school. In the late summer and early fall, those fields are laden with tobacco plants that bend and nod in the gentle wind. Dark green, veined, and leafy, they cover the expanse of the countryside. The fields themselves are framed with a line of trees, which grow so closely together they appear to be an inky smudge. It is lovely to me. When autumn arrives, the harvest arrives as well. The harvesting happens quickly with a flurry of machines and passing trucks, transporting bundles of leaves. In an instant, it seems, the fields are bare. The first time I beheld this seasonal happening, I believed the brown-tilled earth was there to stay until next summer, and I must admit I was mourning the absence of the tobacco plants.

Autumn gave way to winter. In January, the fields, which had been dormant and bare for the last few months, were tinged with a vibrant green. Each day, as I drove past them, the brilliance of the green intensified. I was struck with wonder at what was occurring. Having spent my whole life "up north," where things turned brown in the fall and stayed that way until spring, I was deeply intrigued at what was stirring in those formerly tobacco-filled fields. Dazzling yellow green was covering those fields like a verdant living carpet. I couldn't get over what was happening. Every day as I drove past those fields after picking up the kids from school, I would exclaim to my children, as if it were the first time I'd seen it, "Look at that grass! Isn't it beautiful!"

"Yes, Mommy," they replied, surveying me as though I were slightly unstable.

"Tomorrow I am going to stop at those fields and take a picture and see what the grass looks like up close," I informed them.

"Yes, Mommy," they said with mounting concern. The next day, as I had forewarned them, I circled the car back and pulled off right next to one of those lovely fields. At that very moment, the sun regarded us with clear, rich light, emanating from a brilliantly blue sky, wisps of clouds filling out the firmament. But it was the green grass that was truly spectacular. Saying "green grass" fails on every level to give it justice. C. S. Lewis described the earth we live in as the Shadowlands, a reflection of the world to come, as sky is reflected in water in a beautiful, but somewhat-diminished fashion. On that day, I was convinced the sky and the grass were the real thing. They were the true and living thing, not a mere copy. They seemed alive to me. I shared my musings on the true nature of the grass and sky with my children, who were smiling at me.

"Wouldn't you just love to roll in the grass!" I exclaimed.

"Yes, Mommy." They looked like they were a little worried about me. But mostly, they looked like they were proud of me. I had changed, and they could see it.

As the sun shone warmly on us, standing there at the edge of the field formerly filled with tobacco—which as it turned out was now growing wheat, not just really, really green grass—I knew that change was possible. Because I was changed. My children and I stood marveling at the grass and the sky, how alive they were, how solid and real they looked, how they seemed to be made of stuff that was not the usual stuff of this world. And although we stopped short of actually rolling in the grass, our hearts laughed and reveled in its loveliness. For I was no longer living a sad, imitation of life.

I was living the real thing.

Postscript: Through My Husband's Eyes

BY JOHN EKLUND

It never rains in Arizona.

That's what everyone from the gas station clerk to the Remuda Ranch counselor told me after a torrential downpour flooded the streets of Wickenburg that hot December night. I'd been holed up in a hotel, running back and forth to the residential facility that boasted the highest success rate in the country for patients struggling with eating disorders. My wife was several weeks into a 45 day stay, and I had reluctantly flown out to participate in something Remuda called "family week."

I booked the flight out, grumbled through the rental car reservation, gritted my teeth looking over the directions and agenda sent by Remuda. Why in the world did I have to take time out of my life, steal away from my children, and rob the church of hours I could be spending in ministry? There were people in the world who wanted and appreciated my help. This was my wife's issue. I didn't have the problem. She did.

I'd sent her to these "specialists" so they'd fix whatever was broken inside of her. I'd done my part. I'd paid my dues with Jennene; it was her turn to wrestle with this thing like I had for the length of our marriage. I was angry at Remuda for pressuring me to visit, angry at myself for saying "yes" to going, and angry at my wife for pulling me into her dysfunctional world.

Sitting in the Pittsburgh airport in early December, I tried to prepare for the next 7 days of untold mental and emotional gymnastics. I was built to manage crises. As a therapist and counselor, I was well equipped to bring calm, solution-based thinking to the most desperate circumstances. But when it came to my own family, my own wife, I was a lost, agitated, panic-filled basket case.

I let the rage well up in me unabated, unhindered. I'd spent half of my life stuffing down my feelings. She didn't care how I felt or what I felt—she only knew how she felt. In an effort to keep our four daughters informed, but not fearful, about Jennene's month-and-a-half trip to the desert, we had told them that *mom was really sad and she was getting some help trying to be happy again.* Well, we were all sad… especially me. Where was my seven week stay in a recovery resort?

Jennene's parents stayed with me at the house intermittently throughout her time away. They did their best to bring normalcy to the holiday season for their grandkids, but it was a season of strained smiles. Our laughter would catch itself on guilt and worry like a loose thread on a sweater, unraveling the joy of the season. The shame of enjoying the kids and the life Jennene and I had built would come crashing down on our fragmented family. We'd forget and remember, forget and remember. Voices would trail off unexpectedly; we'd catch each other staring off mid-stir over a batch of Christmas cookies. It was hours of unacknowledged mourning and desperate unanswered prayers.

I soldiered on through my favorite holiday, pretending, losing myself in the girls' joy of the season. But the dark clouds inevitably rolled in—she was ruining it all. Rudolph and Home Alone and Bing Crosby crooning on the radio were all drowned out by the static of her selfish absence. Intense fury bordering on hate was a new emotion I was getting acquainted with. Rage and deep sorrow created a cocktail I was simultaneously drunk and hung over on as the days stretched on without my wife. All of these feelings, wrapped up in a terrifying future and a damaged past, would overwhelm me as sleigh bells jingled and misfit toys found a home.

Jennene had hit her bottom, sending shock-waves through a carefully constructed church existence I reinforced over 6 years of full-time ministry. The mess she made was not just a reflection of the destructive habit she had maintained in secret. Her failure was a reflection of my own glaring inability to perform the work I provided to my church and community within the four walls of my own home. Her failure was my failure. I had taken great care, as a pastor, to look the part of a man in control of his family. Paul's question in 1 Timothy dug at me: *"if a man cannot manage his own household, how can he take care of God's church?"* Didn't she know how bad a light her issues cast on me? Didn't she realize how much damage control her self-indulgent choices required?

Now here I was, taking more time off work, tossing more energy and resources on the altar of her eating disorder.

Maybe this time though…

There it was, groping about in the darkness, a weak flicker of hope that stubbornly believed things might actually improve after her stay. She might get better.

Better. Wow. What would that look like?

From the honeymoon on, my marriage had been like riding down a class 5 rapid without a guide or paddles. Sure, there had been a few moments of still water, but they were few and far between. I had worn myself out trying to hold on while keeping everyone else in the boat safe and relatively happy. I had mastered the art of explaining my wife's isolation, mood swings, odd and ever-changing eating habits and emaciated appearance to everyone from casual church acquaintances to my own daughters.

"She's just a little tired."

"She's not feeling well."

"Don't worry, every couple fights now and again."

"We are both trying this new vegan thing. We've never felt better!"

"Sorry Jennene couldn't make it. She was up late with one of our daughters."

"I wish I had her metabolism!"

"I am not sure if she had dinner… you girls go ahead."

What would it be like to just leave in the morning, confident she wouldn't make herself throw up all day? What would it be like to head out with the kids in tow, secure in the knowledge that she wouldn't lay under the covers, sick and depressed, for the next 6 or 7 hours? I couldn't count the number of times she had pleaded with me, sobbing as I readied myself for work. "Don't leave me," she'd beg. I had to make up new stories for various bosses and coworkers to explain my frequent tardiness. I will never forget the shame (and strange relief) that came over me when my supervisor at a VA internship didn't buy my lame excuse about traffic. He forced a true confession of the mess I left at home. He looked at me with compassion and asked me what he could do to help. I nearly broke down in his office at the gesture, but as always, I merely told him I would handle it.

I could fix it.

Fixing it proved beyond me, and that was where most of the anger came from. From day one of family week at Remuda Ranch, my anger reared its head. Like a golf outing on a busy day, they made us pair up into foursomes for counseling. We acclimated quickly to the arrangement with help from our immensely patient and gifted therapist. He was annoyingly competent. As I was, myself, a Licensed Clinical Social Worker, I was skeptical he could bring anything to the table I hadn't seen or tried on others (or my wife) before. Surprised by his skill and my own eagerness to share, I found myself engaging in the treatment process. I labored through the joint therapy sessions, I scrambled up the climbing wall of the trust course, I even drew a picture of my wife's eating disorder in art therapy. It wasn't pretty. Through it all, however, there was one exercise that consumed almost every spare minute of my stay.

Before the end of our first therapy session, our counselor had given us a homework assignment to be completed at the end of the week. It was called "Truth in Love." Each of us were supposed to write out, in detail, the ways in which we had been hurt by our spouse. We would share it with one another in one of the last meetings. I took to this project like a man possessed. I wrote furiously under the bedside lamp late into the evening at my hotel. I wrote early in the morning over hot coffee at a local restaurant. I even wrote in the rental car between activities throughout the day. I wanted my "Truth in Love" to be a thorough, unfiltered, and long-remembered testament of my pain. It would be a history of the many injustices I suffered. It would speak with great eloquence and authority of the lengths I had gone to keep peace in a home occupied by a tyrant.

My eagerness was borne from a latent exasperation, not just with Jennene, but with myself. I was ultimately embarrassed that I had been so ineffective in helping my own wife progress in her struggle. I was anxious to show someone, anyone, my laundry list of interventions and resources. Now, I would have an audience to the infinite care and compassion, tears, time, and tools I had invested into my wife and marriage. I could expose the ingratitude, spite and abuse of this woman—this was, sadly, the fuel that kept me chugging through family week.

The days ran together in a slow, shuffling march towards the finish line. We were putting one foot in front of the other, trusting the process. Unfortunately, none of us, not the therapist, Jennene, or myself, could admit to seeing much progress. I had learned a few things about disordered eating and had bought into the program more than I intended. However, it was the same old defeated, despairing Jennene I would say goodnight to as the winter sun set over the scrub and sand.

Towards the end of those seven days, I felt my own desperation mounting. This was supposed to be the silver bullet that would kill the monster. More like a golden bullet—45 days in the top eating disorder clinic in the nation was not cheap, and a lot of people had sacrificed to get her here. What was her problem? Didn't she see how hard this was for me, for the kids, for everyone? She was so selfish! How could she so coldly dismiss all the encouragement and support being sent her way? How could she ignore the fact that destroying herself meant destroying the family who loved her?

After one long, difficult and unproductive day of family therapy, I sped away from the ranch in the opposite direction of my hotel. I couldn't face sitting in that spare, banal room all night, flipping through the cable channels, mind filled with malice and loathing. Brooding behind the wheel of my rental car, I crept down the center of Wickenburg proper. It has a quaint and charming downtown with cowboy hats topping the lampposts and life-size statues of various western figures—an old-timey school teacher, luggage in hand, waits endlessly for a ride to her final destination, a cowboy and a lady, dressed for the dance hall, carry on a wooden conversation, a prospector and his donkey lumber down the sidewalk, dreams of discovery eternally frustrated. A few days earlier, I nearly had a coronary when I almost stepped on a life-like bronze rattlesnake while jogging down Frontier St. But the most famous statue of all, displayed with both natural and artificial timelessness in the center of town, is the Jail Tree.

The Jail Tree is a historical reality played out in one outdoor act. Chained to a 200 hundred year old Mesquite sits a forlorn figure of a man in a striped prison uniform, head in his hand. The man's face tells the tale—he is tied to this tree against his will, trapped indefinitely by a combination of bad luck and bad decisions. How did he end up in this stupid one-horse backwater hellhole? I felt the midsize sedan's interior closing in on me as I drifted past the ghostly prisoner. How had I ended up in this God-forsaken place?

God had certainly forsaken me, my marriage, and my children. How many times had I prayed over my wife as she sobbed through another soul splintering apology over purging, or secret spending, or unpredictable rage against me and the kids? Where was this rescue, this ever-present help in time of need I had preached passionately and faithfully about in sermons? Had I not served Him devoutly enough? Was there some past or present sin of mine chaining me to this solitary confinement? I was rolling slowly down the very center of the valley of the shadow of death, and I was alone.

It was all so unfair. So unfair. Where was the justice? Where was my payoff for the thousands of hours of purgatory I toiled through in my relationship with this miserably fragile creature? Had I not shown a worthiness beyond her own sin? I had paid the cost. Was I not a worthy enough sacrifice? What more did God require for her healing?

Pounding the dashboard with my fist, I fought against the overwhelming sadness and loneliness pulling at me, clawing at me.

"I can't do this alone! Why did You do this to me? I am doing my part- why won't You help me?"

I bellowed and roared, my voice absorbed into the cheap upholstery. The road blurred in front of me as I let loose the emotions I had beaten back. I drifted aimlessly through town, not caring where the steering wheel carried me. Maybe I'd just park right here, right in the middle of the road, until the police or the white-coats came and carried me away. As I braked, stationary midway through an intersection, something hit the windshield hard.

It started with one, then two, then an explosion of water drops the size and speed of a thousand hummingbirds. Rain like I'd never seen emptied itself onto the unyielding streets of Wickenburg, flooding every avenue and alley. I just sat there, mouth open, hands at 10 and 2, driver and car paused between both lanes of Tegner Street like a modern addition to the town's collection of aimless statue residents.

I stared at the rivers gushing over the hood, over the benches and awnings, over the curbs and over all of creation. I sat in my little metal cocoon, dry and unaffected. While the rain percussed, unrelenting against the sheet metal of the hood and roof, reality began to avail itself to my ungenerous heart. My wife was dying, and the fact that I couldn't save her was not hurting me, it wasn't scaring me—it was embarrassing me. That's what was happening.

How does a man, powerless to save all he has ever wanted and cared about, respond to a growing realization of his own inadequacy? He writes a list. The "Truth in Love" assignment was lying next to me in the passenger seat. I had her sins ever near me, adding to them line by line, page by page. It had become my greatest comfort through the week. With ever furious scribbles, I was building a case against the woman I made a great show of defending. Windshield rivulets ran their fingers over the loose papers lying beside me, distorting every indictment against my wife.

Jennene confessed her eating disorder to me early in our dating relationship in college. I convinced her to see a counselor on campus of the small Christian University we were attending. When she agreed, I experienced a deep inner satisfaction believing, a) she was going to immediately get better, and b) she would owe it all to me. When, after a mere two sessions, she declared that the therapist was an imbecile and refused to continue, my education into the intricacies of the disorder and into my own impotency in helping her began.

With each failed attempt at saving my wife, I would more acutely feel my own weakness. An aching insecurity grew in me as years of unwillingness or inability to change spat in the face of my magnanimous help. "What's wrong with her?" blended grotesquely with "What's wrong with me?" Over the years, this created another monster more hideous than the disordered eating. An evil that dwarfed the danger that brought my wife to treatment. An evil described by C.S. Lewis as "the Great Sin" in *Mere Christianity*:

> How is it that people who are quite obviously eaten up with Pride can say they believe in God and appear to themselves very religious? I am afraid it means they are worshipping an imaginary God. They theoretically admit themselves to be nothing in the presence of this phantom God, but are really all the time imagining how He approves of them and thinks them far better than ordinary people: that is, they pay a pennyworth of imaginary humility to Him and get out of it a pound's worth of Pride towards their fellowmen.

It was pride.

Degenerate, mean-spirited, deceitful, pharisaical pride was creating and perpetuating the misery in me. I knew it to be true—I always had, but denial is a potent liquor for drowning reason as well as sorrow. I was in denial of how my pride had deprived Jennene of my love and acceptance. I was in denial of how I used her faults to fill the coffers of my own self-righteousness. I enjoyed reclining high upon the light end of the sin scale. My goodness was built on the back of her shame and disgrace.

This list, this "Truth in Love" sat neatly in the co-pilot position of my rental car, carrying neither truth nor love between the folds of its many pages. What I had written was a manifesto—a manifesto of a codependent. Codependency is as dark and demanding as

any addiction and as deeply dug-in as any neurosis. As Dr. Henry
Cloud recently wrote,

> Codependency occurs when we don't have an accurate awareness
> of our boundaries and behaviors, and we allow someone else's
> needs to control and take over our lives.

The Christian love I made a show of exhibiting had been long
ago hollowed out by bitterness and resentment, creating an empty
shell, a dry husk of a former compassion. In codependency, control
becomes a counterfeit to care. My efforts to control and bring relief
to Jennene were, in reality, efforts to take control of my own life, to
bring relief to me.

The truth of this was cemented a day after the deluge of rain
on the streets of Wickenburg. The core intentions of my codependency—to expose, not protect or heal my wife—would explode
the long awaited reading of the "Truth in Love" assignment. Each
of the four of us in our therapy group would bring out our papers
and let loose over a hundred combined years of resentment in one
sitting. I was selected to read last, and so I waited restlessly through
a wife's cutting critique of her husband's inadequacy, and then
through a husband's tearful outpouring of his wife's dirty laundry as
she shook sobbing knee to knee with her accuser.

They embraced and apologized profusely in a hundred nauseating sentiments as Jennene timidly pulled out her papers. I had felt
my resolve weaken slightly in the authenticity of the former couple's
sharing. His reluctance to inflict pain and her shattered response at
his recitation had me questioning my vehemence. My softening was
short-lived, however, as my wife began to move through her list.

She felt demeaned and patronized when I played the therapist.

She felt judged and condemned when I played the pastor.

She felt isolated and abandoned by my growing apathy.

She said my anger broke her, and it made her want to give up.

Really? My anger broke her? She had never seen real anger. It was building in me like a fire. With each syllable of her "Truth in Love", the rage within me grew. Unleashing the raw, unfiltered story of this woman's insanity, and my heroic efforts to defend her, rescue her, deliver her would more than exonerate me—it would redeem me.

It was my turn. My eyes fell on the papers, the writing... I took a deep breath. Before a word could pass my lips, I heard the therapist say, *"I'm sorry John, we are out of time."*

"What? No, no. No it's my turn."

"We just don't have the time. We need to wrap up."

"I wrote all this. What am I supposed to... what about all this?"

"I'm sorry. We need to move on."

Move on. But this is how I planned to move on.

I don't really remember how I got out of that chair, smiled at the other couple, and put one foot in front of the other while gripping all that was unread and unsaid as I walked out the door. Some of my quiet malice was directed towards our therapist, but it carried no weight, and faded almost as soon as I felt it. There was a familiar flash of hate towards my wife, but it was stale, tasteless, and suddenly unsatisfying. It would seem appropriate to shake a fist at heaven, yet it was all too clear, too abundantly clear to ignore. This was the hand of God raised against me, and I was defeated. His grace towards my wife had magnificently won. He had protected her from me. And in doing so, He had protected me from myself.

This was the beginning of my own recovery, my own fight against the usurper in me. That day, I was refused entry into a world of self-justification and self-pity that would have been my undoing. I will forever be grateful.

It's taken another half-decade to understand the significance of this divine intervention. A door God shut tight was my salvation. I didn't see it that way at the time, but I now identify it as my moment of clarity amidst the blood-lust of my codependency. I was convinced that my wife would get better only when she fully understood her guilt. The guilt of her sin against me. The guilt of her sin against the girls. The guilt of her sin against God. But that's not how it works, is it? Grace says, while we were yet sinners, Christ died for us. Guilt and shame had kept Jennene enslaved. It was grace that would set her free... and free her it did.

I needed to fly all the way across the country to an eating disorder facility in the desert to find grace. It was an outpouring of grace in the desert—grace like rain.

And it never rains in Arizona.

About the Author

Jennene Eklund is a wife, a mom of four daughters(!), a sometimes volleyball coach, a survivor, and a fighter for freedom. She has experienced recovery from a twenty year battle with eating disorders and shame. She would love for you to know what freedom feels like, too. Whether your struggle is with food or fear or depression or addiction or religious condemnation- victory is possible.

You can find Jennene online at **jenneneeklund.com.**

If you would like to learn more about
Celebrate Recovery, check out the book
Your First Step to Celebrate Recovery
(available at pastors.com) or visit
www.celebraterecovery.com.